2C

New
MANHATTAN
Restaurants

The Food Enthusiast's
Long Weekend Guide

Andrew Delaplaine

Andrew Delaplaine is the Food Enthusiast.
When he's not playing tennis,
he dines anonymously
at the Publisher's expense.

Senior Editor – James Cubby

MANHATTAN

The Food Enthusiast's Complete Restaurant Guide

Table of Contents

INTRODUCTION

There's a whole world of distinct neighborhoods in Manhattan. A whole wonderful world. Believe me, I have walked them all and enjoyed every minute of it (except when it was raining, and sometimes, even then).

For the purposes of this book, I am dividing the listings into 4 sections, Downtown, Midtown, Upper East Side and Upper West Side. But everybody knows there's much more to it than that.

EAST SIDE vs WEST SIDE

Fifth Avenue divides East from West. Anything east of Fifth Avenue is on the East Side; anything west is, well, you get it. The puzzling part assaults newcomers when they get down to 14th Street, where Downtown really begins. Here you get streets that are not numbered as much as named. Mott Street, Canal, Houston, Bleecker, etc. This gets very confusing.

AVENUE ADDRESSES

The great avenues of Manhattan are not as glamorous as the ones in Paris, but they are important because they are the main arteries that run north and south. The street address on an "avenue" means nothing to the outsider. You need to know the "cross street" to be able to locate it. That's why in the listings below, you'll see something like "1234 Lexington Ave (bet. 30th and 31st Sts)," which tells you where it is without you having to pull out your cell phone and resort to Google Maps, which, by the way, you'll find extremely helpful as you navigate your way around Manhattan.

MIDTOWN

Strictly speaking, Midtown runs from 34th Street to 59th Street, where Central Park begins. (For newbies, 59th Street is also called Central Park South.)

Downtown, most people agree, really starts at 14th Street. There's a great amount of wonderful activity going on between 14th Street and 34th Street, which is neither a part of Downtown, nor a part of Midtown. (I personally call it LoMi, for Lower Midtown, but nobody else does.)

In this book, however, I am including this "in between" area in the Midtown section. This includes neighborhoods like the Flower District, Hudson Yards, Kips Bay, NoMad, Chelsea, Gramercy Park (one of the many places I lived in New York), Union Square, the famous Meatpacking District, and others.

Midtown is divided between **Midtown West** and **Midtown East**, with, as I said above, Fifth Avenue being the dividing point.

DOWNTOWN

14th Street south. This takes many varied neighborhoods—Greenwich Village (East Village and West Village), Lower East Side, Nolita/NoLiTa, SoHo, Little Australia, Little Italy, Chinatown, the Financial District and a whole lot more. As noted above, I'm including LoMi in this section.

UPPER WEST SIDE

The Upper West Side really is Central Park West to the Hudson River, and from 59th Street up to 110th Street. When you hear the term "Upper Manhattan," it means the area north of 96th Street.

West Harlem runs from 125th Street to 155th Street. And it goes on and on.

UPPER EAST SIDE

Just as there is with the Upper West Side, the Upper East Side has several different neighborhoods. To a New Yorker, the Upper East Side means the area between 59th Street to 96th Street. East Harlem begins there and runs up to 141st Street, from Fifth Avenue east to the river. Within this is Yorkville (79th to 96th), Carnegie Hill (86th to 98th), and still others.

It's not as daunting as it sounds. But this is a BIG city, and it takes time to learn the many neighborhoods that make it up.

Chapter 1
DOWNTOWN

ANTON'S
570 Hudson St (bet. 11th St & Perry St), 212-924-
0818
www.antonsnyc.com
CUISINE: American (Traditional) / Wine Bar /
Italian
DRINKS: Full bar
SERVING: Dinner nightly; Lunch also Fri – Sun.
PRICE RANGE: $$$
NEIGHBORHOOD: West Village

A cozy little café and wine bar with a simple but very good menu. Old-school New York atmosphere, one of those places in the Village where it's just as welcoming whether you slip in for a lovely dinner in the little room, or drop in at the bar for a nightcap on your way home. This part of town has buildings that are human scale, so the whole neighborhood is very comfortable. The building dates from 1850. Some seating outside in good weather. Favorites: Chopped chicken liver & hearts (I love this dish, though a lot of people recoil at the very idea of it); Spinach Ravioli drizzled with sage butter; Pork Rib Chop (expertly grilled); and the Hanger Steak. Nice wine selection.

ATERA
77 Worth St (Church St), 212-226-1444.
www.ateranyc.com
CUISINE: New American
DRINKS: Full bar; wine paring available.
SERVING: Tues-Sat only. Single seating at 6:30. Takes 3 hours. (Reserve 2 months out for weekend seating)
Prix fixe menu only, costing several hundred dollars per person if you get the wine parings. Only 13 chairs per night (plus a single table).
NEIGHBORHOOD: TriBeCa
PRICE RANGE: $$$$
You'll get whatever the chef wants to make the night you visit. (They "present" the menu to you, but only at the end of your visit.) With 20 or so courses, you won't be disappointed. You get to watch all this from your perch on a bar stool where you see them make the food with a reverence that almost seems to be too

much. They put the plate in front of you and you wonder if you're supposed to bow to it or eat it. Eat it.

BABBO
110 Waverly Pl (bet. N Washington Sq & Mac Dougal St), 212-777-0303
www.babbonyc.com
CUISINE: Italian
DRINKS: Full Bar

SERVING: Dinner, Lunch (Tues – Sat)
PRICE RANGE: $$$$
NEIGHBORHOOD: Greenwich Village
High-end Italian eatery of Mario Batali's located in a
repurposed carriage house. Great welcoming
atmosphere. Menu favorites: Spicy two-minute
Calamari; Barbecued skirt steak; Lamb chops.
Extensive menu. Make reservations.

BALTHAZAR
80 Spring St (bet. Crosby St & Broadway), 212-965-
1414
www.balthazarny.com
CUISINE: French
DRINKS: Full Bar
SERVING: Breakfast, Lunch & Dinner
PRICE RANGE: $$$
NEIGHBORHOOD: SoHo
Iconic French brasserie featuring classy interior and
impressive menu and a winning crowd with lots of
buzz about it. Bobby Flay says he likes the steak
frites and coq au vin here. Another great chef, Eric
Ripert, likes the steak frites, too, but says, "I go as
often as I can—they have great energy, good service,
and fantastic steak frites." Other Menu picks: French
toast with bacon and Chicken Liver & Foie Gras
Mousse. Great dining experience. A favorite for any
meal.

BAR BELLY (Formerly Lead Belly)
14B Orchard St (bet. Canal St & Hester St), 917-488-
0943
www.barbellynyc.com

CUISINE: Seafood
DRINKS: Full Bar
SERVING: Dinner; closed Sundays
PRICE RANGE: $$
NEIGHBORHOOD: Chinatown, Lower East Side
Popular neighborhood eatery (almost no tourists) with a purposeful down market shabby look. Great seafood selection. Crowded on weekends. Happy hour specials (oysters and craft cocktails expertly rendered by the gifted bartenders). Live music and DJ.

BATARD
239 West Broadway (bet. Walker St & Beach St), 212-219-2777
www.batardtribeca.com
CUISINE: Modern European/American (New)/French
DRINKS: Full Bar
SERVING: Dinner; Closed Sun
PRICE RANGE: $$$$
NEIGHBORHOOD: TriBeCa
Those of you with long memories will recognize that Batard's location is more famous than it is, having once housed such culinary stars as Corton and, going back to 1985, Montrachet. This was where Daniel

Boulud got his start. This place has seen the neighborhood change over the years, becoming what might now be considered the most interesting part of Manhattan to live or work in. Batard today is an upscale eatery offering a creative menu of European, American and French cuisine. One thing about it that is so impressive is the quality of its food without the pretentiousness found in so many other places. The wine list is a wonderful example of the best quality with fair prices. Lots of great selections from Alsace, Austria, Germany, but a great selection of red and white Burgundy. Favorites: Black bass with roasted shrimp & fennel, Octopus is beautifully prepared, the Duck exquisite. Braised pork shoulder with savoy cabbage surprisingly lighter than it sounds. Great presentation. Delicious desserts.

THE BEATRICE INN
285 W 12th St (bet. 4th St & 8th Ave), 212-675-2808
www.thebeatriceinn.com
CUISINE: American (Traditional)/Seafood
DRINKS: Full Bar
SERVING: Dinner; closed Mondays
PRICE RANGE: $$$
NEIGHBORHOOD: West Village
Vanity Fair editor Graydon Carter (or is it Carter Graydon?) opened this little upscale chophouse and the celebrities flocked. Great atmosphere, especially in the winter when the fireplace is lit. They touch all the bases, from the opening round of expertly created craft cocktails through to the stunning desserts. Favorites: Roast Duck flambé and Milk braised pork

shoulder. Ideal for a very special celebration.
Reservations recommended.

BUBBY'S
120 Hudson St, 212-219-0666
www.bubbys.com
CUISINE: American
DRINKS: Full Bar
SERVING: Breakfast, Lunch, Dinner
PRICE RANGE: $$
NEIGHBORHOOD: Tribeca
Known for its traditional American cuisine, here
everything is made from scratch using traditional
family recipes. Menu favorites include: Pulled pork
and Fried chicken – each order comes with the
restaurant's signature buttermilk biscuits. For dessert
there's a selection of home-baked pies and cakes.

BUDDAKAN
75 9th Ave (nr. W 16th St) 212-989-6699
www.buddakannyc.com
CUISINE: Chinese/Asian Fusion
DRINKS: Full Bar
SERVING: Dinner
PRICE RANGE: $$$
NEIGHBORHOOD: Meatpacking District, Chelsea
Of course, in Chinatown, you get the "most
authentic" Chinese food, but this place in Chelsea
comes mighty close to the best of the best if you're
looking for authenticity. Large, lavishly decorated
eatery offering an impressive menu of Asian fare.
Favorites: Glazed Alaskan black cod and Monk fish.
Creative cocktails. A luxurious dining experience.

CARBONE
181 Thompson St (bet. Houston St & Bleecker St),
212-254-3000

www.carbonenewyork.com

CUISINE: Italian

DRINKS: Full Bar

SERVING: Lunch & Dinner; Dinner only on Sat &
Sun

PRICE RANGE: $$$$

NEIGHBORHOOD: Greenwich Village

High-end Italian eatery that attracts the A-list crowd,
making it one of the toughest spots to secure a table.
(Don't order too much—portions are generous.) The
veal parmigiana is the size of a hubcap. This is one of
the few places where they make Caesar salad
tableside (remember when they used to do that
everywhere?), so you can always get more anchovies
right away without having to send the waiter back to
the kitchen later. Beautiful & fun dining experience.
When you first enter, it's tight and packed, but this
soon gives way to 3 dining rooms. Tourists arrive

early, and locals come in later, but the vibe at all times is very welcoming. Menu picks: Burrata with Eggplant caponata and Veal parmesan. Superior wine list, with some 250 selections, about half Italian. Book ahead.

CHARLIE BIRD
5 King St (nr. Houston St), with entrance on 6th Avenue, 212-235-7133
www.charliebirdnyc.com
CUISINE: Italian
DRINKS: Full Bar
SERVING: Lunch & Dinner
PRICE RANGE: $$$
NEIGHBORHOOD: border of SoHo & West Village
This two-level eatery offers New American fare with a heavy Italian twist. Fried squash blossoms stuffed with cheese and anchovies are an amuse bouche; Chicken liver; Cappellacci pasta topped with puree of peas and guanciale; crispy-skinned chicken cooked under a brick is delectable; and the Veal Chop. Standout dessert is the molten chocolate cake. Nice wine selection (tilted toward Italy) has about 120 selections, all quite good. About 40 of them are priced under $100.

CROSBY STREET BAR
79 Crosby St (bet. Prince & Spring Sts), 212-226-6400
www.firmdalehotels.com
CUISINE: American
DRINKS: Full Bar
SERVING: Breakfast, Lunch, Dinner
PRICE RANGE: $$$$
NEIGHBORHOOD: SoHo
Located on a quiet cobblestoned street in the **Crosby Street Hotel**, this bar, in addition to its funky British charm, features classic English afternoon tea. The menu is creative but the portions are small. The bar offers specialty cocktails and an international wine list. Outdoor seating available. (Be sure to slip into the bathroom for a look at the wallpaper.)

DISTILLED
211 W Broadway (at Franklin St), 646-809-9490

www.distilledny.com
CUISINE: American (with many twists)
DRINKS: Full bar; creative cocktails
SERVING: Dinner nightly; brunch on weekends
NEIGHBORHOOD: TriBeCa
PRICE RANGE: $$

The wide round wheel-like chandeliers hanging from the very high ceiling in here make you gasp for a second when you walk in. I remember seeing similar gargoyle-type wagon wheels in steakhouses in my youth. But these are fun.

The dark woods and cozy booths give off a warm feeling, and so does the staff.

Lots of whimsical twists on classic pub fare: chicken wings, yes, but amped up with gochujang and chili paste; a BLT, yes, but with sunflower sprouts, slivers of bacon, basil and tomatoes on sourdough; onion rings, yes, but fried, frozen and then fried again.

The burger is made with grass-fed beef, but my favorite is the duck they treat like chicken: it's breaded and fried. (I can honestly say I've never had it prepared so simply. I thought it would be dry, but it was succulent.)

A lot of other little twists and turns on the menu, but all of them exciting and unexpected. A fun place you'll love.

ESTELA
47 E Houston St (bet. Greene St & Mulberry St), 212-219-7693
www.estelanyc.com
CUISINE: American (New)

DRINKS: Full Bar
SERVING: Dinner; Lunch Fri - Sun
PRICE RANGE: $$$
NEIGHBORHOOD: Nolita, NoHo
Popular eatery serving small plates of American fare
with a Mediterranean twist. Favorites: Beef tartare
with sunchoke and Grilled foie gras and grape leaf.
Intimate dining experience. Nice wine selection.

ESSEX MARKET
88 Essex St (Cor. Essex & Delancey Sts), no phone
https://www.essexmarket.nyc/
CUISINE: Food Court
DRINKS: Full bar
SERVING: 7 a.m. – 1 a.m.
PRICE RANGE: $$-$$$

NEIGHBORHOOD: Lower East Side
This is an historic market, opened originally in 1940 to house many of the vendors that had pushcarts along the crowded streets of the Lower East Side. They've had to move into different buildings over the years, and this is the newest, so you'd never know the history of the Market by just walking in here. There's a 90-minute walking & tasting tour Tuesday night and Saturday morning, from Turnstile Tours, https://turnstiletours.com/ I took it one rainy afternoon and it was a lot of fun. Essex has lots of vendors offering nearly everything. GROCERY (Luna Brothers Fruit, Luis Meat Market, etc.); SPECIALTY (Formaggio Essex, Olive & Spice, Tops Hops, Café d'Avignon (bakery), Japanese Deli & more; PREPARED FOODS (such as Arancini Brothers, offering Sicilian street food, Puebla Mexican Food, Dominican Cravings, Don Ceviche, Mille Nonne offering Italian cuisine, Zerza, with Moroccan food, etc.). Downstairs you'll find the **MARKET LINE**, which has another batch of vendors offering even more. www.marketline.nyc You can see how real New Yorkers live and shop when you visit a place like this.

FAIRFAX
234 W 4th St (bet. 10th St & Charles St), 212-933-1824
www.fairfax.nyc
CUISINE: Café/Wine Bar
DRINKS: Full Bar
SERVING: Breakfast, Lunch, & Dinner
PRICE RANGE: $$$

NEIGHBORHOOD: West Village
This all-day café (part coffee shop/part wine bar) offers a menu of Mediterranean small plates. There's a well-worn leather sofa in the corner with a couple of huge chunks of marble in front of it where I like to relax with drinks. Favorites: Soft poached eggs and soldiers (strips of cheesy bread) and Carbonara Flatbread. The omelets are cooked in the French style—light, fluffy, perfect. Great choice for brunch.

GATO

324 Lafayette St (bet. Houston St & Bleecker St), 212-334-6400
www.gatonyc.com
CUISINE: Mediterranean/Spanish
DRINKS: Full Bar
SERVING: Dinner
PRICE RANGE: $$$
NEIGHBORHOOD: NoHo
Hip eatery (one of Bobby Flay's) in a huge ballroom-sized location. Flay is actually from New York, so this is yet another homecoming. This incarnation of Flay's is like a cross between his shuttered Mesa Grill and his Bolo spot. While the menu here is described as "New Mediterranean," it's more influenced by Spain than any other cuisine. The huge bar is always packed three-deep it seems, but the bar is the place to be to enjoy the bite-sized plates and tapas dishes. The simple wooden tables and café-style cane chairs throw off a casual vibe. The music cranks up the later the evening gets, which is why I prefer to go a little early. The colorful brick walls and floor tiles make the sound seem much louder. Favorites: Ricotta &

plum crostini; artichoke and wild mushroom paella; mussel & clam salad; chorizo crépinette; I particularly liked the white anchovies topped with a dollop of sour orange sauce; squid rings with bacon bits sprinkled on top also are very good. Nice dessert selection.

GOTHAM BAR & GRILL
12 E 12th St (bet. 5th Ave & University Pl), 212-620-4020
www.gothambarandgrill.com
CUISINE: American (New)
DRINKS: Full Bar
SERVING: Lunch, & Dinner, Dinner only on Sat & Sun
PRICE RANGE: $$$$
NEIGHBORHOOD: Union Square/Greenwich Village

A romantic fixture (for over 3 decades) offering a menu of New American classics in a big open room on a quiet Village street. You can look down into the dining room from a big long bar on the left side of the room that's raised a couple of steps. The lampshades that look like parachutes cast a lovely glow while jazz quietly plays in the background. Favorites: Roast Niman Ranch Pork and Soft-Shell Crabs. Try the key-lime pie served with ice cream.

GREEN GARDEN VILLAGE
216 Grand St (bet. Mott St & Elizabeth St), 646-912-9136
https://www.greengardenvillageny.com/
CUISINE: Dim Sum/Noodles/ Cantonese
DRINKS: No Booze
SERVING: Breakfast, Lunch, Dinner
PRICE RANGE: $$
NEIGHBORHOOD: Little Italy
The Duck is their specialty but their menu impresses. Favorites: BBQ Pork and Alaskan King Crab. Most dishes served family style. Great atmosphere – like an old style Chinatown eatery.

HARRY'S CAFÉ & STEAK
1 Hanover Sq (bet. William St & Stone St), 212-785-9200
www.harrysnyc.com
CUISINE: Steakhouse
DRINKS: Full Bar
SERVING: Lunch, & Dinner; Closed Sun
PRICE RANGE: $$$
NEIGHBORHOOD: Financial District

Popular and very comfortable steakhouse with an adjoining café. Harry's has been around for decades and it remains a wonderful place prized by first-timers and the hundreds of locals that come here regularly. Lots of nooks and crannies as well as platforms which are great for people-watching. Solid food, great portions, perfect to satisfy a hearty appetite. The menu has changed a little to reflect the shift in population in the area, so now besides the typical NYC steakhouse fare, you can get things like seafood tacos. But don't. This place has been known for its wonderful steaks, its raw bar and its Caesar salad, so get a steak, like the 20-oz bone-in strip, a 16-oz Cajun rib eye, a prime hanger steak. French onion soup is great.

HIGH STREET ON HUDSON
637 Hudson St (bet. Gansevoort St & Horatio St), 917-388-3944
www.highstreetonhudson.com
CUISINE: American (New)
DRINKS: Full Bar
SERVING: Breakfast, Lunch, & Dinner
PRICE RANGE: $$
NEIGHBORHOOD: West Village
Popular Philly spin-off eatery offering a menu of seasonal American cuisine. This is one of those places where you wish you lived on the same block, because you'd enjoy it whether you came here for breakfast, lunch or dinner. If you did live on the same block, you'd be here several times a week, different times of the day. The in-house bakery accounts for the delicious breads and pastries. For b'fast, get the

Hickory Town sandwich with Lancaster bologna, fried egg and pickled mayo. At lunch, try the duck meatball sub. For dinner, try the honey-glazed chicken with the chicken skin Caesar salad. Or grilled fish.

I SODI
105 Christopher St (bet. Bedford St & Bleecker St), 212-414-5774
www.isodinyc.com
CUISINE: Tuscan
DRINKS: Full Bar
SERVING: Dinner
PRICE RANGE: $$$
NEIGHBORHOOD: West Village
Intimate, romantic eatery (only 8 or 9 tables and some bar stools) with a long bar on one side and tables on the other. Food is firmly rooted in Tuscany. Don't expect dishes from any other part of Italy, which makes this place so damned wonderful—it is what it is, and what it is is perfect. The pastas here are top-notch and the portions are large. I like the tortelli made with chestnut flour and stuffed with chestnuts or the ravioli filled with ricotta & spinach. Tagliata (grilled sirloin) is excellent; the Cornish game hen cooked under a cast iron weight is sublime, with the thinnest possible breading giving a crackle to the skin when you bite into it; the lasagna will melt in your mouth. Wine list is a trifle high-priced.

IL BUCO ALIMENTARIE & VINERIA

53 Great Jones St. (bet. Bowery & Lafayette St.),
New York: 212-837-2622.
https://ilbuco.com/pages/alimentari
CUISINE: Italian
DRINKS: Beer & wine
SERVING: Lunch, dinner
NEIGHBORHOOD: NoHo
PRICE RANGE: $$-$$$
The copper, the imported tiles from Italy, the
communal tables of wood all combine to make you
feel like you're in the Old Country. The Market in the
front offers all kinds of artisanal things for sale, but
it's the aromas escaping from the open kitchen in the
back (redolent with some from wood they use to cook
with) is what you'll want to focus on. Seasonal menu,
so it changes, but expect things like short ribs, rabbit
fried and sauced, crispy polenta, porchetta alla

Romana. Donna Leonard, who has **Il Buco** over at 47 Bond St., set this place up.

KATZ'S DELICATESSEN
205 E. Houston St. (at Ludlow St.), 212-254-2246
www.katzsdelicatessen.com
CUISINE: Deli, Sandwiches
DRINKS: Beer & Wine
SERVING: Breakfast, Lunch, Dinner
NEIGHBORHOOD: Lower East Side
PRICE RANGE: $$
Of course, there's nothing quite like Katz's Deli anywhere. If you want to have a corned beef or pastrami sandwich in New York, have it here. (The knoblewurst with its pungent garlic and fat is also an excellent choice, but so are the potato latkes.) You think you've been in a Jewish Deli—you haven't till you've been here. Also excellent because of the colorful clientele. Open since 1888. $$

L'ATELIER DE JOEL ROBUCHON
85 Tenth Ave (bet. Ave of the Americas & 5th Ave), 212-488-8885
www.joelrobuchonusa.com
CUISINE: French
DRINKS: Full Bar
SERVING: Dinner; Closed Sun & Mon
PRICE RANGE: $$$$
NEIGHBORHOOD: Meatpacking District, Chelsea
Wildly expensive upscale eatery with a big U-shaped dining counter that looks onto the kitchen. You sit on red leather stools. There are a few tables against the wall for bigger groups. Fine modern French cuisine

and tasting menus. Favorites: Wagyu beef, King crab in avocado cannelloni, Veal sweetbreads; Veal cheeks confit "blanquette-style"; and Sliders crowned with a dab of foie gras. Beautiful spot for romantic or special occasions. Finish things off with an excellent chocolate soufflé.

LAFAYETTE GRAND CAFÉ & BAKERY
380 Lafayette St (bet. 4th St & Great Jones St), 212-533-3000
www.lafayetteny.com
CUISINE: French/Bakery
DRINKS: Full Bar
SERVING: Breakfast, Lunch & Dinner
PRICE RANGE: $$$
NEIGHBORHOOD: NoHo
Belle Epoque-style brasserie/bakery combination serving classic French fare: beef tartare with watercress & a quail egg; delicate butter lettuce with Roquefort, country ham and a tangy herb vinaigrette; one of the best steak frites in town. The impressive selection of bakery confections make it a favorite for breakfast as well. Delicious pastas.

LOCANDA VERDE
Greenwich Hotel
377 Greenwich St. (at N. Moore St.), New York: 212-925-3797
www.locandaverdenyc.com
CUISINE: Italian, American
DRINKS: Full bar
SERVING: Lunch, Dinner

NEIGHBORHOOD: TriBeCa
PRICE RANGE: $$$
Robert De Niro is partnered with star **Chef Andrew Carmellini** to bring you this hip trendy spot. Casual comfort food exceedingly good: go for a pasta dish unless you're there when they offer fried chicken. Chocolate donuts for dessert a must.

MARKET LINE
115 Delancey St (corner Norfolk St & Delancey St) – no phone; individual vendors have phones
www.marketline.nyc
CUISINE: Food Court
DRINKS: Full bar
SERVING: 7 a.m. – 1 a.m.
PRICE RANGE: $$
NEIGHBORHOOD: Lower East Side
Located downstairs from the **ESSEX MARKET**, this food collection offers 30 locally-sourced vendors and restaurants. Some of the eateries include: Ukrainian

Diner & Grocer Veselka, family-run German butcher shop and grocer founded in 1937 Schaller & Weber, and 1920s tea parlor and dim sum eatery Nom Wah. Seating in the middle, some of the larger places have their own dining space.

MIMI
185 Sullivan St (bet. Houston St & Bleecker St), 212-418-1260
www.miminyc.com
CUISINE: French
DRINKS: Full Bar
SERVING: Dinner, Lunch only on Sat & Sun
PRICE RANGE: $$$
NEIGHBORHOOD: West Village
Contemporary eatery offering a menu of elaborate French classics (with some modern twists) in a very small bistro on a quiet street in the Village. Favorites: Chicken liver mousse, pot-au-feu (with tuna), Rabbit ballotine with sweet peaches, Sweetbreads with lobster mushrooms, Veal tartare and Clams with Squid. Don't leave without trying the Espresso Martini.

MOMOFUKU MILK BAR
251 E 13th St (near Second Ave), 646-692-4154
www.milkbarstore.com
CUISINE: Bakery, Ice Cream & Frozen Yogurt
DRINKS: No Booze
SERVING: Desserts
PRICE RANGE: $$
NEIGHBORHOOD: East Village

This dessert specialty shop offers a variety of freshly baked cookies, cakes and pies. Popular items include the Confetti Cookie and Cornflake Baking Mixes. Specialty favorites include Cereal Milk (milk that tastes like it was poured from a bowl of cereal). Small lunch menu available. Novelty items for sale like T-shirts, bags, and cookbooks.

MOMOFUKU SSÄM BAR
89 South Street, Pier 17, 212-254-3500
www.momofuku.com/new-york/ssam-bar/
CUISINE: Korean, American
DRINKS: Full bar
SERVING: Lunch, Dinner
NEIGHBORHOOD: Seaport
PRICE RANGE: $$$
Pork buns, pork buns, pork buns. Braised goat also a winner. Smart crowd here, loud and bustling. Loads

of fun. There's that special excitement that is New York in this place.

MIGHTY QUINN'S BARBECUE
103 Second Av. (nr. 6th St.), 212-677-3733
www.mightyquinnsbbq.com
CUISINE: BBQ / Southern
DRINKS: Beer & Wine
SERVING: Lunch, Dinner
NEIGHBORHOOD: East Village
PRICE RANGE: $
Sustainable smoked meats. They started with a little street side stand and now have a roof over their heads. Get the sweet potato casserole with maple syrup and pecans.

MISSION CHINESE FOOD
171 E Broadway, New York: 917-376-5660
www.missionchinesefood.com
CUISINE: Chinese
DRINKS: Full bar
SERVING: Lunch, Fri-Tues, 12-3; dinner, Thurs-Tues, from 5:30. Reserve on missionresy@gmail.com
NEIGHBORHOOD: Lower East Side
PRICE RANGE: $$
Chef Danny Bowien started in San Francisco, but he's made quite a splash here, wowing all the critics and attracting a sophisticated crowd to this little joint. Salt cod fried rice, beef brisket, cumin lamb breast, catfish.

MORANDI
211 Waverly Pl (bet. Charles St & 10th St), 212-627-7575
www.morandiny.com
CUISINE: Italian
DRINKS: Full Bar
SERVING: Breakfast, Lunch & Dinner
PRICE RANGE: $$$
NEIGHBORHOOD: West Village
Rustic trattoria serving an impressive menu of Italian cuisine that attracts Chef Bobby Flay more than any other eatery in town. Menu picks: Gnocchi with pancetta and Tagliatelle Bolognese. Impressive wine and cocktail selection. Sidewalk seating.

MOTORINO
349 E 12th St (bet. 1st Ave & 2nd Ave), 212-777-2644
www.motorinopizza.com
CUISINE: Pizza/Italian
DRINKS: Beer & Wine Only
SERVING: Lunch & Dinner
PRICE RANGE: $$
NEIGHBORHOOD: East Village
Small eatery serving great pizza (also delivers) and Italian fare. The pizza here is Neapolitan in style and his big blistered crusts. Usually a wait as it's always busy.

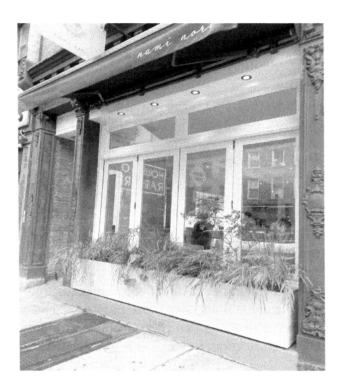

NAMI NORI

33 Carmine St (bet. Ave of the Americas & Bedford St), 646-998-4588

www.naminori.nyc

CUISINE: Japanese / Temaki Bar

DRINKS: Beer & Wine

SERVING: Lunch & Dinner, Dinner only on Sat; Closed Sundays

PRICE RANGE: $$

NEIGHBORHOOD: West Village

In a light and airy room, you'll find this minimalist hand-roll eatery offering an impressive selection. Favorites: Spicy crab Dynamite and Lobster tempura. You must try the furikaké fries with tomato tonkatsu.

Vegetarian options. So simple, basic, cheerful … very well done. Mostly bar seating but turn-around is fast.

NARCISSA
25 Cooper Sq (bet. Bowery & 4th St), 212-228-3344
www.narcissarestaurant.com **WEBSITE DOWN AT PRESSTIME**
CUISINE: American (New)
DRINKS: Full Bar
SERVING: Dinner, Lunch on Sat & Sun
PRICE RANGE: $$$
NEIGHBORHOOD: East Village
Next to the Standard Hotel is this popular upscale eatery offering a menu of refined, farm-to-table New American cuisine. The succulent baby chickens from the rotisserie are famous. Two dining rooms and an open kitchen. Private garden open weather permitting. Limited wine selection. Reservations recommended.

NOWON
507 E 6th St (bet. Ave B & Ave A), 646-692-3867
www.nowonnyc.com

CUISINE: Korean/American (New)
DRINKS: Beer & Wine
SERVING: Dinner
PRICE RANGE: $$
NEIGHBORHOOD: East Village, Alphabet City
Small eatery serving interesting combos that must be
tried to believe. Favorites: Honey Butter tater tots;
Octopus & Spam Fried Rice; Sizzling Kimchi Rice.

PORTALE
126 W 18th St (bet. 7th Ave & Ave of the Americas),
917-781-0255
www.portalerestaurant.com
CUISINE: Italian
DRINKS: Full bar
SERVING: Dinner
PRICE RANGE: $$$
NEIGHBORHOOD: Chelsea
Comfortable eatery offering Italian/American fare in
a very cozy room with distressed wooden planks
painted white lining one wall. The place was filled
with a fun, busy crowd when I came in with a friend
to escape a nasty winter night. Favorites: Foie Gras
Tortellini; Mushroom Risotto. Try the Meatball
Sliders and you'll be hooked. Delicious gelati for
dessert. Nice bar scene.

RAOUL'S
180 Prince St (near Sullivan St), 212-966-3518
www.raouls.com
CUISINE: French
DRINKS: Full Bar
SERVING: Dinner

PRICE RANGE: $$$
NEIGHBORHOOD: South Village
This intimate neighborhood gem offers a nice menu
with tasty authentic French bistro dishes like steak
frites (their signature dish). Delicious desserts like
crème brûlée.

ROSEMARY'S
18 Greenwich Av., New York: 212-647-1818
http://rosemarysnyc.com/
CUISINE: Italian
DRINKS: Beer & Wine
SERVING: Breakfast, Lunch, Dinner, Brunch; no
reservations except for parties of 8+.
NEIGHBORHOOD: Greenwich Village
PRICE RANGE: $$
Named after the boss's mother, this place maintains a
garden on the rooftop of the building. Homemade
pastas. A cute little place. Wine list has $40 bottles;

by the glass for $10. Lamb, porchettina, braised pork shoulder.

RUSS AND DAUGHTERS
179 E Houston St (bet. E Houston St & 2nd Ave), 212-475-4880
www.russanddaughters.com
CUISINE: Smokehouse
DRINKS: No Booze
SERVING: Breakfast, Lunch, & Dinner
PRICE RANGE: $$
NEIGHBORHOOD: Lower East Side
A NYC institution since 1914 (and still owned by the same family) serving quality smoked fish, homemade pickled lox, traditional baked goods, smoked sturgeon, whole smoked trout, herring, whitefish and other specialty foods. Their bagels are famous. You walk in here and the first thing you do is grab a number by the door and with for it to be called. The wait is always worth it. You can taste anything they have before you order it. There aren't many stores like this left in New York. (They were called "appetizing" stores because they were formed based on Kosher rules—if you wanted meat, you went to a delicatessen; if you wanted fish or cream cheese or bagels, you went to an "appetizing" store.)

SOHO DINER
Soho Grand Hotel
320 W Broadway (bet. Canal St & Grand St) 212-965-3011
www.sohodinernyc.com
CUISINE: Diner

DRINKS: Full Bar
SERVING: Open 24 hours
PRICE RANGE: $$
NEIGHBORHOOD: South Village, TriBeCa
Diner atmosphere in the Soho Grand Hotel serving "elevated diner fare," which means it costs a little more than a regular diner (but not really). The portions are substantial. And the place is clean as a

whistle. Since it's open 24 hours, I stumble-bumble my way in here if I'm in this part of town late at night and have had too much to drink (this happens occasionally)—I always get the same thing, the Egg Sandwich, with 2 eggs on a Kaiser roll with tomato aioli. (The bacon is extra, but get it—it really makes this sandwich stand out.) Then off to bed. It's good, it's quick, it's cheap. Menu picks: Rigatoni Bolognese; and Ham Steak & Eggs with chimichurri.

Large menu (75 items) but no substitutions. Cocktails and old-school sodas. Jukebox plays vinyl.

THE SMILE
26 Bond St (near Lafayette St), 646-370-1446
www.thesmilenyc.com
CUISINE: American
DRINKS: Full Bar
SERVING: Lunch, Dinner, Brunch
PRICE RANGE: $$
NEIGHBORHOOD: NoHo / Washington Square
Popular among the young, artsy crowd, this coffee shop style restaurant offers a rustic yet friendly atmosphere just east of Washington Square. Menu favorites include: Egg-ham-Gruyère-and-caramelized-onion sandwich and Baked eggs with tomato, Manchego, and avocado. Wine list, mostly French, is small but moderately priced.

TEMPLE COURT
The Beekman Hotel
5 Beekman St (bet. Nassau St & Theatre Aly), 212-658-1848
www.templecourtnyc.com
CUISINE: Steakhouse/Gastropub
DRINKS: Full Bar
SERVING: Breakfast, Lunch, & Dinner
PRICE RANGE: $$$
NEIGHBORHOOD: Financial District
Located in the landmark Beekman hotel, south of the Brooklyn Bridge on-ramp, is this American restaurant offering an impressive menu. The restaurant takes its name from the building, which was called Temple

Court, built in 1881, before it became the Beekman. The bar is a great experience, in a large open room with an atrium that rises 9 floors. The dining room is very luxe, with ornate embellishments, rich with leather, stained glass, deep polished woods, glittering chandeliers. Favorites: Duck a l'orange with baby fennel and Agnolotti, Monkfish with a hint of wood smoke, Spanish prawns with heads on, set off with roasted mushrooms and greens, Loin of lamb enhanced with lemon confit. The wine list is suitably impressive, but way overpriced. I drank Scotch the last time I was there, saving my party a good $300 to $500 by skipping the wine. Great desserts.

TRIBECA GRILL
375 Greenwich St. (at Franklin St.), New York: 212-941-3900

www.myriadrestaurantgroup.com
CUISINE: American
DRINKS: Full bar
SERVING: Lunch, Dinner
NEIGHBORHOOD: TriBeCa
PRICE RANGE: $$$
They've developed a wildly supportive and sophisticated following. Maine lobster salad makes a good starter; Long Island duck breast, pan-roasted pork chop. Busy and fun bar scene.

WALLSÉ
344 W. 11ᵗʰ St. (at Washington St.), New York: 212-352-2300
www.kurtgutenbrunner.com/restaurants/wallse/
CUISINE: Austrian
DRINKS: Full bar
SERVING: Dinner nightly; Brunch on Sunday.
NEIGHBORHOOD: West Village

PRICE RANGE: $$$
Poached Maine Lobster with Quark Spaetzle;
Viennese beef (sometimes oxtail) Goulash with sour
cream; beef strip loin with crispy onions; lobster
ravioli. In a perfectly wonderful setting that you think
of when you think of Old New York: a tree-lined
cobblestoned street.

WAVERLY INN
16 Bank St (bet. Waverly Pl & 4th St), 917-828-1154
www.waverlynyc.com
CUISINE: Steakhouse/Gastropub
DRINKS: Full Bar
SERVING: Breakfast, Lunch, & Dinner
PRICE RANGE: $$$
NEIGHBORHOOD: West Village
Upscale eatery offering a creative menu of American
comfort fare, steaks and oysters. Don't let the hype
scare you away. (The hype is getting a little tired
anyway.) Just because it's owned by former "Vanity
Fair" editor Graydon Carter and has the image of a
place where celebrities rule, people like you and me
really *can* get a table here. Cocktails served in a
clubby atmosphere on a quiet residential street in the
Village. This is one of those quintessentially New
York restaurants that I love so much, because it's
loud, boisterous and everybody seems to be having
such a good time. The leather banquettes, the low
lighting, the pictures of famous guests. In the
bathroom there are paintings of zebras and George
Gershwin at the piano smoking a cigar. Try the Black
Truffle Mac & Cheese, the Filet steak Diane, Jonah
crabcakes with more crab than breading, an excellent

burger. Almost like a downtown Joe Allen. Nice choice for date night.

WOLFGANG'S STEAKHOUSE
409 Greenwich St (bet. Beach St & Hubert St), 212-925-0350
www.wolfgangssteakhouse.net
CUISINE: Steakhouse
DRINKS: Full Bar
SERVING: Lunch & Dinner
PRICE RANGE: $$$$
NEIGHBORHOOD: Tribeca
Elegant high-end steakhouse that has an "old New York" atmosphere you'll revel in. Everybody pretty

much agrees Wolfgang stole Peter Lugar's act, tweaked it, and brought it to Manhattan. Some even say his waiters are gruffer than those crusty old coots at Lugar's. My favorite: the exquisite Porterhouse steak. The requisite nice selection of wines. Seafood and vegetarian options available.

ZZ'S CLAM BAR
169 Thompson St (bet. Houston St & Bleecker St), 212-254-3000
www.zzsclambar.com
CUISINE: Seafood
DRINKS: Full Bar
SERVING: Dinner; closed Sunday & Monday
PRICE RANGE: $$$$
NEIGHBORHOOD: Greenwich Village
Hip, hot spot serving an impressive menu of seafood and raw bar specialties. Favorites: Tuna carpaccio with foie gras and Apple cocktail with shiso and basil. Raw oysters are perfection. Reservations only.

Downtown
Budget Spots

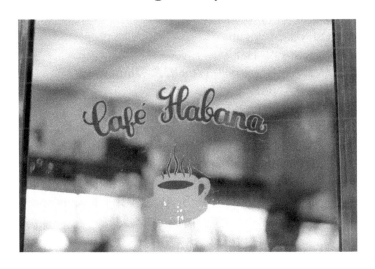

CAFÉ HABANA
17 Prince St (at Elizabeth St), New York: 212-625-2001
www.cafehabana.com/
CUISINE: Cuban, Mexican
DRINKS: Full bar
SERVING: Lunch, Dinner
NEIGHBORHOOD: NoLita
PRICE RANGE: $$

Hip little eatery with great food inspired by the Café Habana in Mexico City, not Havana. Tortas or burritos: Eggs with chorizo, grilled steak, Sloppy Joe BBQ pork sandwich, chicken Diablo, great soups. The Cuban sandwich here was voted best in New York.

EMPELLON AL PASTOR
132 St Marks Pl (bet. Avenue A & 1st Ave), 646-833-7039
www.empellon.com
CUISINE: Mexican
DRINKS: Full Bar
SERVING: Breakfast, Lunch, & Dinner
PRICE RANGE: $
NEIGHBORHOOD: East Village
Offshoot of Empellón, this sister eatery offers a cheap taco-focused menu that happens to be very good indeed. Order from the counter at the far end of the busy bar. Favorites: Breakfast burrito (served only at dinner, oddly enough), Baby Back Rib Carnitas and Chicken Nuggets. Tasty margaritas.

HANOI HOUSE
119 Saint Marks Pl, 212-995-5010
www.hanoihousenyc.com
CUISINE: Vietnamese
DRINKS: Beer & Wine Only
SERVING: Dinner nightly, Lunch only on Sat
PRICE RANGE: $$
NEIGHBORHOOD: East Village, Alphabet City
Comfortable eatery offering a limited menu of Vietnamese fare. Favorites: Spicy Octopus, Bun cha

with meatballs slightly charred wrapped in betel leaves, Bo luc lac (filet mignon with honey, soy & butter), Crispy Spring Rolls so good you could eat a dozen of them.

Chapter 2
MIDTOWN
East & West

15 EAST
15 E 15th St, 212-647-0015
www.15eastrestaurant.com
CUISINE: Japanese, Sushi
DRINKS: Full bar
SERVING: Lunch, Dinner (except Sun., when closed)
NEIGHBORHOOD: Union Square, Flatiron
PRICE RANGE: $$$$
Chef Masato Shimizu oversees this sushi bar offering some of the best sushi in the city. Raves continue for this place. Why the sake is better here than anywhere else I'll never understand. (I hate sake, but all my friends insist this is the case here.)

ABC KITCHEN

35 E 18th St (bet. Broadway & Park Ave S), 212-475-5829

www.abchome.com/eat/abc-kitchen

CUISINE: American, French

DRINKS: Full bar

SERVING: lunch weekdays, dinner nightly, brunch on weekends from 11.

NEIGHBORHOOD: Midtown South

PRICE RANGE: $$$

They're very conscious about their organic offerings here, which is highly unusual for a place that really cares about sustainable foods that also attracts a high-powered (and very stylish) crowd. The chef picks up produce from the nearby Union Square Greenmarket. Cheerful setting in a bright clean spot with old rustic beams saved from a crumbling barn that give the place some "texture." Pasta with greens, poached egg and lemon crumbs, calamari (the breading is crushed pretzels), ricotta cavatelli with shrimp and tomatoes. Whole wheat wood-fired pizzas are a specialty here: tomato, mozzarella, basil; or the fennel sausage,

tomato, broccoli; or the clams, mint, parsley. Roast
suckling pig with braised turnips a consistent winner.

ABURIYA KINNOSUKE
213 E 45th St (Third Ave), 212-867-5454
No Website
CUISINE: Izakaya/Japanese
DRINKS: Full Bar
SERVING: Lunch & Dinner, Dinner only Sat & Sun
PRICE RANGE: $$$
NEIGHBORHOOD: Midtown East
Upscale eatery offering a menu of authentic Japanese
izakaya cuisine. It doesn't get better than this, folks.
My Favorites: Miso Black Cod; Koji-marinated
chicken; and the excellent Fried Capelin Fish. Like
dining in Tokyo. Nice selection of sakes.

AI FIORI
Langham Hotel
400 Fifth Ave (bet. 37th St & 36th St) 212-613-8660
www.aifiorinyc.com
CUISINE: Italian/French
DRINKS: Full Bar
SERVING: Breakfast, Lunch, & Dinner
PRICE RANGE: $$$$
NEIGHBORHOOD: Midtown East
Upscale eatery offering gourmet fare from the Italian
and French Riviera, combining Italian ingredients
with French technical mastery. Food, while rich, is
not "heavy" in the way things used to be. Favorites:
Braised Lamb; Veal-stuffed agnolotti in a rich
mushroom sauce; Sea scallops gently charred;
Lobster poached in butter; excellent Duck.

Reservations a must. Ideal choice for a special occasion. Impressive selection of regional wines. In fact, one of the best wine lists in a city with lots of them. Over 2,000 selections. Italian reds are particularly noteworthy for the depth in their list. (Over 130 Champagnes are carried.)

ARETSKY'S PATROON
160 E 46th St (bet Lexington Ave & 3rd Ave), 212-883-7373
https://aretskyspatroon.com/
CUISINE: German
DRINKS: Full Bar
SERVING: Lunch, Dinner
PRICE RANGE: $$$
NEIGHBORHOOD: Midtown East
Located in a charming four-story Manhattan townhouse, this place makes every meal a celebration and even hosts rooftop cocktails. The menu consists of seasonal American favorites. Menu favorites

include: 5-day Dry Aged Rib eye and Salmon with quinoa and yogurt sauce. Try the delicious creative cocktails and desserts (yummy chocolate cake and homemade ice cream).

ARMANI RISTORANTE
717 Fifth Ave, 212-207-1902
www.armani.com/restaurant/us/restaurant/armani-ristorante-5th-av/
CUISINE: Italian
DRINKS: Full bar
SERVING: Mon – Sat, lunch and dinner; only brunch on Sun
NEIGHBORHOOD: Midtown East
PRICE RANGE: $$$
This swank eatery is on the second floor of the Armani store on Fifth Avenue, hence the name. Everything is happily Italian, from the sleek waiters (clad in Armani, of course) to the fine wine list. (Don't worry, there are some bottles for less than $45).

The place is chic and slick as befitting Armani himself, who actually owns the place. That said, the price level is not $$$$, but $$$. Some of the dishes here are actually bargains when you consider the high quality on display.

You might opt for the bone-in veal chop Milanese (since that's where Armani is from). It's beyond perfection. Other hearty choices are the osso buco and the delectable cotoletta de vitello.

I got out without touching a dessert, but they looked spectacular.

AQUAVIT

65 E 55th St (bet. Madison and Park), 212-307-7311
www.aquavit.org
CUISINE: Scandinavian
DRINKS: Full bar
SERVING: Lunch, Dinner
NEIGHBORHOOD: Midtown South
PRICE RANGE: $$$$

Long a respected entry among top-rated Manhattan restaurants, here in this cool, subdued atmosphere you'll get to experience really interesting food. For lunch, try the Swedish meatballs or gravlax from the a la carte menu. There's a 4-course prix fixe menu at dinner or a 7-course tasting menu.

BENIHANA

47 W 56th St (Ave of the Americas), 212-581-0930
benihana.com
CUISINE: Japanese/Sushi
DRINKS: Full Bar
SERVING: Lunch & Dinner
PRICE RANGE: $$$
NEIGHBORHOOD: Midtown West

Well-known Hibachi chain serving Japanese dishes grilled tableside. Did you know this is the original Benihana from 1964? I did. For many (somewhat older) Americans, a Benihana was the first place they ever used chopsticks. The first place they ever tasted sake. Dining experience is theatrical and fun making it popular with tourists. It's too "dated" for me these days because there are SO many more options where you can get Japanese food (and far better than the ordinary stuff they serve here). Buy if you've never

been to a Benihana or have kids, this is a good bet.
Favorites: Hibachi shrimp and Teriyaki Steak.

BENOIT
60 W 55th St (bet. Fifth & Sixth Aves), 646-943-7373
www.benoitny.com
CUISINE: French
DRINKS: Full Bar
SERVING: Lunch & Dinner
PRICE RANGE: $$$
NEIGHBORHOOD: Midtown
One of Midtown's popular spots for a "power lunch,"
this is a great place for lunch or dinner. Menu
favorites include: Duck and Foie Gras Terrine with
Pear and Apple Chutney and Traditional Cassoulet
with Bacon, Sausage, Belly, and Duck Confit.
Delicious desserts. (Try to nab a table in the bar
area—much more interesting than the dining room.)

BURGER JOINT
Le Parker Meridian Hotel

119 W 56th St (bet. Sixth & Seventh Aves), 212-708-7414
www.burgerjointny.com
CUISINE: American, Burgers
DRINKS: Beer & Wine
SERVING: Lunch & Dinner
PRICE RANGE: $$
NEIGHBORHOOD: Midtown West
Located in Le Parker Meridian Hotel. Just follow the neon burger sign and you'll find this cute little burger joint behind velvet curtains in the lobby. Here you'll find a simple menu of burgers, fries and milkshakes but everything is tasty. And for New York, cheap.

CAFÉ AT AKA CENTRAL PARK
42 W 58th St (near Fifth Ave), 646-744-3104
www.stayaka.com
CUISINE: Gourmet Cafe
DRINKS: Full Bar
SERVING: Breakfast & Lunch
PRICE RANGE: $$
NEIGHBORHOOD: Midtown
Located in the Hotel Central Park, this café serves breakfast and lunch all day. Menu favorites include Lemon Ricotta pancakes and Smoked Salmon scrambled eggs. Everything here is made with fresh ingredients from local farms. The décor is chic and modern giving it an upscale café ambiance.

COSME
35 E 21st St (bet. Broadway & Park Ave South), 212-913-9659
www.cosmenyc.com

CUISINE: Mexican
DRINKS: Full Bar
SERVING: Lunch & Dinner
PRICE RANGE: $$$
NEIGHBORHOOD: Flatiron
Popular Mexican eatery serving locally sourced small-plates. Menu picks: Duck carnitas and Stuffed avocado. Most Mexican food made in America is just slop. Not here. Very subtle things going on. Take a bite of the tortillas served on the side and you'll realize the kind of crapy tortillas you've had before and thought were "Mexican." Great selection of artisanal spirits. Churros prepared to perfection for dessert.

CRAFT
43 E 19th St (bet. Park Ave S. & Broadway), 212-780-0880
www.craftrestaurantsinc.com/
CUISINE: American
DRINKS: Full bar
SERVING: Dinner from 5:30
NEIGHBORHOOD: Flatiron District
PRICE RANGE: $$$$
Soft-shell crabs if they have them. The best. Otherwise, loin of rabbit, braised short ribs, a 30-day dry-aged sirloin served with bone marrow, pork ravioli.

DECO FOOD + DRINK
231 W 39th St (bet. 7th Ave & 8th Ave), 646-993-1650
https://thedeconewyork.com
CUISINE: Food Court
DRINKS: Full bar
SERVING: Breakfast, Lunch, and Dinner
PRICE RANGE: $$$
NEIGHBORHOOD: Garment District / Midtown West
Art Deco inspired food hall that celebrates the many cultures of New York offering a variety of cuisines including Mexican, Afghan, French rotisserie, Hawaiian rotisserie, Brazilian, Roman Pizza, French, Sandwiches, and Pastries. Lots of varied seating choices, from communal tables to single tables to a

lounge-like area with comfortable plush chairs and coffee tables.

DEL FRISCO'S DOUBLE EAGLE STEAK HOUSE
1221 Ave of the Americas (near 48th St), 212-575-5129
www.delfriscos.com
CUISINE: Steakhouse/American (New)/Seafood
DRINKS: Full Bar
SERVING: Lunch & Dinner
PRICE RANGE: $$$$
NEIGHBORHOOD: Theater District, Midtown West
Luxurious chain eatery specializing focusing on steaks and seafood. The big dining space is 3-stories and very dramatic with its dominating bar. Written into the dark wood is a motto: "Do Right & Fear No Man." The wine list is perhaps the very best among ALL New York steakhouses, and its exhaustive selection of California cabernets is the deepest of ANY New York restaurant. Favorites: Filet medallions or any of the prime steak cuts, Pan-seared salmon from the Bay of Fundy, Roasted chicken that's tender and juicy, Lobster Mac and Cheese. Signature cocktails. Everything is good. Reservations recommended.

DOCKS OYSTER BAR
633 Third Ave, 212-986-8080
www.docksoysterbar.com/
CUISINE: Seafood
DRINKS: Full bar
SERVING: Lunch, Dinner, Brunch
NEIGHBORHOOD: Murray Hill; Midtown South
PRICE RANGE: $$$$
All things seafood. Steamer clams, lobster, pan
roasted Dover sole, Maine lobster risotto, seafood
gumbo, maki and hand rolls, great raw bar. If you
can't get to the Oyster Bar in Grand Central, come
here instead.

ELEVEN MADISON PARK
11 Madison Ave, 212-889-0905
www.elevenmadisonpark.com/
CUISINE: American, French
DRINKS: Full bar
SERVING: Lunch, Dinner
NEIGHBORHOOD: Flatiron District

PRICE RANGE: $$$$
They jumped to a fixed-price multi-course (mostly French) menu to shake things up a while ago, so it's God knows what by now for the whole meal. This is one of the most celebrated restaurants in New York, if a little fussy and self-important. If you show up in a bad mood, the over-enthusiastic staff will cheer you up, as will the stupendous food. (It's not fun to come here, but it's interesting.)

EMPELLON
510 Madison Ave (bet. 52nd St & 53rd St), 212-380-1215
www.empellon.com
CUISINE: Mexican
DRINKS: Full Bar
SERVING: Breakfast, Lunch, & Dinner; open 24 hours
PRICE RANGE: $$$
NEIGHBORHOOD: Midtown East
Excellent upscale Spanish eatery. Favorites: Gnocchi and Skirt steak. Impressive wine selection.

FRESCO BY SCOTTO
34 E 52nd St (Fifth Ave), 212-935-3434
frescobyscotto.com
CUISINE: Italian
DRINKS: Full Bar
SERVING: Lunch & Dinner, Dinner only on Sat; Closed Sun & Mon
PRICE RANGE: $$$
NEIGHBORHOOD: Midtown East

Family-run upscale eatery offering a menu of authentic Tuscan cuisine that's been here for years. Music gets a little loud for my taste only because they ramp it up too early. The place has always had a lot of regulars from the neighborhood, which is always a good sign. Favorites: a Frito Misto here that I adore; Clam Spaghettini; an Eggplant & Zucchini parm that's stupendous (I don't see this combination many other places—it's inspired here); a Lasagne that's one of the most popular entrées on this fine menu. Authentic Italian pizza. Desserts include homemade Italian cheesecake and real cannoli.

GALLAGHERS STEAKHOUSE
228 W 52nd St (Broadway), 212-586-5000
gallaghersnysteakhouse.com
CUISINE: Steakhouse/American Traditional
DRINKS: Full Bar
SERVING: Lunch & Dinner
PRICE RANGE: $$$$
NEIGHBORHOOD: Midtown West
This well-known steakhouse founded by former Ziegfeld girl and a colorful gambler has for many years been one of my favorite steak joints in the city. I'm always excited when I slip in here and squeeze up to the always busy bar, where within 5 minutes I meet several people. Lots of locals, not as many tourists as a lot of places in this part of town. Known as the only steakhouse in NYC that grills their steaks over hickory coals. Typical meal is salad, mashed potatoes, Porterhouse steak and chocolate cake. I skip the chocolate cake, however, and always start with the Baked Clams Oreganata and I switch out the mashed

potatoes for the Lyonnaise. The food here is simple and delicious. The genuine crowd of "real" New Yorkers creates an atmosphere that is heady, fun and makes you wish you never moved out of town. Reservations recommended.

GRAMERCY TAVERN
42 E 20th St (bet. Broadway & S Park Ave), 212-477-0777
www.gramercytavern.com
CUISINE: American (New)
DRINKS: Full Bar
SERVING: Lunch & Dinner
PRICE RANGE: $$$$
NEIGHBORHOOD: Flatiron
Well known tavern featuring a wonderful fixed-price-only menu as well as great a la carte choices. This bar is one of the most fun and busiest in New York. The more casual tavern up front gives way to a more expensive dining room in the rear, so you get to choose from 2 different experiences. People even dress differently in the 2 rooms. But either one is great. Favorites: Duck breast & sausage, Grilled shrimp & dumplings, Corn tortellini, Pea shoot salad and their famed burger. Very good vegetarian dishes available. Great dessert selection. Favorites: Busy bar scene. Creative desserts – try the cookie tray.

**GRAND CENTRAL OYSTER BAR &
RESTAURANT**
89 E 42nd St, Grand Central Terminal, lower level,
212-490-6650
oysterbarny.com
CUISINE: Seafood
DRINKS: Full Bar
SERVING: Lunch & Dinner; Closed Sat & Sun
PRICE RANGE: $$$
NEIGHBORHOOD: Midtown East
You must eat here at least once. This is more than a
restaurant. To me, it's a quintessential New York
attraction. And to me, there's nothing remotely
"touristy" about it, though of course you'll find a lot
of tourists here. You'll also find hundreds of business
people making deals and talking loud and in the
process of living in New York. This is what it looks
like. (I eat here every time I'm in the neighborhood,
and I usually am if I'm taking a train out of town).
Iconic eatery serving raw oysters, pan roasts &

chowders in a unique setting of vaulted ceilings covered with white subway tiles. The noise created with all the conversation bouncing off the white tiles is cacophonous and I wouldn't have it any other way. So wonderfully "New York." Fresh oysters like no other place, sometimes offering 30 different varieties. You can also get scallops, clams, lobster, and shellfish. But what I'd recommend is that you order a pan roast (or a stew) from a seat at the pink counter, the one that faces the antique kettles powered by steam. From your perch you can watch as a cook (who's been doing this longer than you think) dips a little butter mixed with clam juice into the kettle, drops in some shellfish that is then covered with half-and-half. After cooking, this wonderful brew is tilted on a hinge into your bowl. You can get it with cherrystones but the absolute best is with oysters.

THE GRILL
99 E 52nd St (bet. Madison Ave & Park Ave), 212-375-9001
www.thegrillnewyork.com
CUISINE: American (Traditional)
DRINKS: Full Bar
SERVING: Dinner; Closed Sun
PRICE RANGE: $$$$
NEIGHBORHOOD: Midtown East
Located in the Seagram Building, this upscale steakhouse serves classic American cuisine. They have a tough act to follow, since this was where the famed Four Seasons was located. You get the feeling that they might be trying too hard, with an emphasis on over-the-top techniques. Is it really necessary for

the roast beef to be sliced tableside? (It's really good, too, with the mustard rub.) The crab cakes are made with no breading at all. Very nice. Pasta la Presse and Prime Rib. Don't leave without trying the Peach Melba (again, prepared tableside). This is an unforgettable dining experience. Impressive wine list.

HAN BAT
53 W 35th St (near Sixth Ave), 212-629-5588
www.nychanbat.com
CUISINE: Korean
DRINKS: Beer & Wine
SERVING: Lunch, Dinner
PRICE RANGE: $$
NEIGHBORHOOD: Koreatown
Very popular Korean eatery. Intimate and often crowded. This 24-hour eatery serves typical Korean fare like crispy pancakes with squid and mandoo, crispy half-moon-shaped dumplings.

HATSUHANA
17 E 48th St (Madison Ave), 212-355-3345

hatsuhana.com
CUISINE: Sushi
DRINKS: Full Bar
SERVING: Lunch & Dinner; Closed Sat & Sun
PRICE RANGE: $$$
NEIGHBORHOOD: Midtown East
Iconic Japanese eatery serving fresh sushi and sashimi. It has the distinction of being the first Japanese eatery to get a 4-star review in the "Times." (That was in 1983 and they're still going strong serving fantastic food.) Favorites: Box of Dreams (comes with 6 types of fish) and Chirashi. You'll want to try the Miso Soup. Reservations recommended.

IPPUDO WESTSIDE
321 W 51st St (bet. 9th Ave & 8th Ave), 212-974-2500
www.ippudony.com
CUISINE: Ramen
DRINKS: Full Bar
SERVING: Lunch & Dinner
PRICE RANGE: $$
NEIGHBORHOOD: Theater District, Midtown West, Hell's Kitchen
Stylish eatery offering a menu of Japanese small plates, ramen and upscale sake. Known for their Ipudo. Other favorites: Maguro tartare and Seasonal Shoyu ramen. Usually packed and there's often a wait.

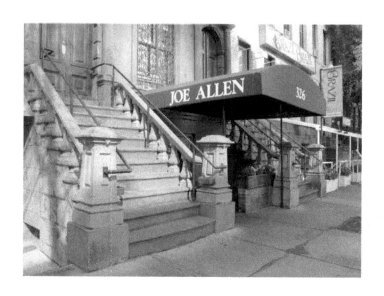

JOE ALLEN

326 W 46th St (bet. Eighth & Ninth Aves.), 212-581-6464

www.joeallenrestaurant.com

CUISINE: American comfort food
DRINKS: full bar
SERVING: lunch, dinner
NEIGHBORHOOD: Midtown West / Theatre District
PRICE RANGE: $$$

As a writer (I write novels and movies as well as travel books), I am at the theatre a lot, and it's a rare visit to New York that I don't slip into Joe Allen for lunch or dinner or in some cases, when I'm pushed for time between a matinee and an evening performance, both. His burger made Joe famous long before burgers were big business. His steak tartare is among the best in town. This is the only place I know that has calf's liver on the menu every day. (Get it with bacon and onions, of course.) Meatloaf and mashed potatoes. Take a look at the Broadway posters on the wall. Ever heard of the shows? Probably not. Joe began the tradition of only putting up posters of shows that were disastrous flops.

JUE LAN CLUB
49 W 20th St (bet. Avenue of the Americas & 5th Ave), 646-524-7409
www.juelanclub.com
CUISINE: Chinese
DRINKS: Full Bar
SERVING: Lunch & Dinner
PRICE RANGE: $$$
NEIGHBORHOOD: Flatiron
Remember the old nightclub Limelight that was housed in a former church? Now it's a glitzy stylish eatery offering a menu of modern (Americanized) Chinese cuisine. There's a garden with lot of shade where you can eat in good weather. Favorites: Chicken kao pao and Wong tong. Great cocktails. Ice cream and sorbet for desserts.

JUNOON
19 W 24th St (bet. Fifth & Sixth Ave), 212-490-2100
www.junoonnyc.com/
CUISINE: Indian
DRINKS: Full bar
SERVING: Lunch, Dinner
NEIGHBORHOOD: Midtown South
PRICE RANGE: $$$
Two dining rooms here, one somewhat Spartan, the other more lavish. You've never had Indian food like

this back home. About the best New York has to offer.

KEENS STEAKHOUSE
72 W 36th St (near Sixth Ave), 212-947-3636.
www.keens.com
CUISINE: Steakhouse
DRINKS: Full bar
SERVING: Lunch, Dinner
NEIGHBORHOOD: Midtown West
PRICE RANGE: $$$$
One of those wonderful New York experiences, open since 1885. They're famous for a huge mutton chop that can feed 4 (but it can't feed 4 if I'm around!). On the dining room ceiling you'll see their collection of churchwarden pipes. The pipes were long and thin and too delicate to be carried in a bag, so patrons left their pipes here to be brought to them when they

finished a meal so they could smoke. Members of Keens's Pipe Club have included everybody from Theodore Roosevelt to Will Rogers and Babe Ruth, architect Stanford White, Douglas MacArthur. With a legendary reputation, this is Manhattan's best-known USDA Prime-only steakhouse. You may know Capital Grille in your hometown, or Morton's or any of many other steakhouses, but in Manhattan, it's Keens. (It's also the oldest steakhouse in the city, and when you walk in, you'll understand what I'm saying: it's like going back in time.) Great décor. For dessert it's almost obligatory to get the classic New York cheesecake. Before Keens was Keens, it was part of the theatrical club called the **Lambs Club**, whose manager was Albert Keen.

KOCHI
652 10th Ave (bet. 45th St & 46th St), 646-478-7308
www.kochinyc.com
CUISINE: Korean
DRINKS: BYOB

SERVING: Dinner; Closed Mondays
PRICE RANGE: $$
NEIGHBORHOOD: Hell's Kitchen, Midtown West
Cozy Korean eatery with an open kitchen offering both *a al carte* and tasting menus. The 9-course tasting meal is a must for newbies. Favorites: Raw scallops and Chicken with aged shitake mushrooms. Reservations recommended. **Note: BYOB.**

L'AMICO
EVENTI HOTEL
849 6th Ave (bet. W 29th & 30th Sts), 212-201-4065
www.lamico.nyc
CUISINE: Italian
DRINKS: Full Bar
SERVING: Lunch, Dinner and weekend brunch
PRICE RANGE: $$
NEIGHBORHOOD: Midtown West
This rustic-chic eatery offers a menu of pizza and creative Italian fare. There are 2 brick ovens sheathed in copper. One is used exclusively to turn out brick-oven pizzas and brunch specials like French toast and Shaksuka. The other is used to finish off chickens and steaks. Attracts a young crowd. They also provide the food for the adjacent Eventi Hotel, with an area that opens onto a big outdoor seating area with a movie screen, available weather permitting.

THE LAMBS CLUB
132 W 44th St, 212-997-5262
www.thelambsclub.com
CUISINE: American
DRINKS: Full Bar
SERVING: Breakfast, Lunch, Dinner
PRICE RANGE: $$$$
NEIGHBORHOOD: Midtown West
This place attracts all kinds of interesting folks, from editors and publishers from Conde Nast and Hearst, execs from HBO (with offices nearby) and Broadway producers looking for angels. They're all dressed very nicely either because they can afford to or because they have to. The chef here offers carefully crafted menus that make dining here a special and often a decadent experience. Menu favorites include: Chicken Cobb salad and Nova Scotia lobster roll. Live jazz every Tuesday and Wednesday, Sunday Jazz Brunch. Check website for special events. This is

one of those rare great restaurants also open for breakfast (get the huevos rancheros).

LE BERNARDIN
155 W 51st St (bet. Sixth & Seventh Ave), 212-554-1515
www.le-bernardin.com
CUISINE: Seafood, French
DRINKS: Full bar
SERVING: Lunch weekdays, Dinner
NEIGHBORHOOD: Midtown West
PRICE RANGE: $$$$
I will always opt for a saddle of lamb or a simple veal chop over any fish when I'm out, but you owe it to yourself to experience the Dover sole here. It's swimming not in water where it was caught, but in butter, sauced so beautifully that it takes your breath away. Melts in your mouth. Everything else about Le Bernardin is sublimity itself. Chef Eric Ripert assumed the duties here (1991) on the untimely death of Gilbert Le Coze who came to New York and showed American chefs a new way to cook that the smartest among them have tried to copy. Ripert stays one-step ahead of them in this beautiful temple to culinary excellence.

LINCOLN RISTORANTE
142 W 65th St, 212-359-6500
www.lincolnristorante.com
CUISINE: Italian
DRINKS: Full Bar
SERVING: Lunch & Dinner
PRICE RANGE: $$$

NEIGHBORHOOD: Upper West Side / Lincoln Center

Right in Lincoln Center, this sleek and modern place is stunning, but the big deal here is not the décor, it's the delicious Italian fare. Menu favorites include: Parpadelle with truffles and lamb served over creamy polenta. Wine list is totally Italian. The chef here, Jonathan Benno, used to work at **Per Se**.

MAREA

240 Central Park S, 212-582-5100
www.marea-nyc.com
CUISINE: Italian/Seafood
DRINKS: Full Bar
SERVING: Lunch & Dinner
PRICE RANGE: $$$$
NEIGHBORHOOD: Midtown West

Upscale (but remarkably unstuffy) Italian eatery offering a menu of superior housemade pastas and seafood. From its sunken dining room, you can gaze at Central Park across the street through the big windows lining the room. There's a quieter dining room behind the busy bar. Newbies should try the Prix Fixe menu to appreciate the full range this kitchen covers. Favorites: Strozzapreti (a seafood medley with lump crab meat, sea urchin and basil over wonderful pasta), Lobster burrata and Steelhead trout. Delicious Italian desserts.

MARTA

29 E 29th St (bet. Madison Ave & Park Ave South), 212-651-3800
www.martamanhattan.com
CUISINE: Italian/Pizza
DRINKS: Full Bar
SERVING: Lunch & Dinner

PRICE RANGE: $$$
NEIGHBORHOOD: Flatiron, Midtown East
Casual eatery in the towering lobby of the **Martha Washington Hotel** known for their cracker-thin pizza and delicious Italian fare. Favorites: Ricotta pizza (Oven-Roasted Peaches, Aged Balsamic, Grilled Sourdough) and Macellaio (Sopressata, Guanciale, Pork Sausage, Mozzarella, Grana Padano); rabbit meatballs; lamb mixed grill. Avoid the main entrees here. Stick with the thoroughly memorable pizza, with the thinnest crust you've ever had, bar none. Start with the rabbit meatballs while you wait for the pizza to cook in those gorgeous ovens behind the counter. Great cocktails. Usually crowded.

MICHAEL'S

24 W 55th St (bet. Avenue of the Americas & Fifth Ave), 212-767-0555
www.michaelsnewyork.com
CUISINE: American
DRINKS: Full Bar
SERVING: Breakfast, Lunch, Dinner
PRICE RANGE: $$$$
NEIGHBORHOOD: Midtown West
Open since 1989, this restaurant has been a popular meeting spot for media moguls and industry insiders. Big shot editors and publishers from "Old Media" lunch here, as well as billionaire real estate tycoons and the like. Nothing special about the décor here. Floral arrangements and a maroon carpet. If you weren't a first-time visitor here, you'd never notice the art on the walls. The best table in the house is #1, an 8-seat table squeezed into the window alcove. Even if you don't recognize who's sitting there, trust me, they are Somebody. Guests dine on a menu featuring haute California cuisine (things like egg white omelets with tomatoes, mushrooms and onions) and slurp down wines from an award-winning list. Menu favorites include: Smoked Salmon Pizza and Long Island Duck Breast.

NIPPON
155 E 52nd St (Third Ave), 212-688-5941
restaurantnippon.com
CUISINE: Japanese/Sushi
DRINKS: Full Bar
SERVING: Lunch & Dinner, Dinner only on Sat; Closed Sun
PRICE RANGE: $$$

NEIGHBORHOOD: Midtown East
With the reputation as the first Japanese restaurant to
serve sushi in NYC (that would be back in 1963),
they have maintained quite a substantial following
ever since. (I'm one of their biggest fans). Favorites:
Yellowtail & Scallion Roll and Shrimp Tempura.
Nice selection of sakes.

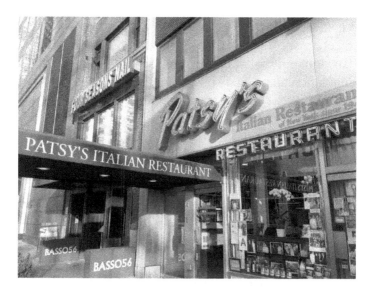

PATSY'S ITALIAN RESTAURANT
236 W 56th St (Eighth Ave), 212-247-3491
patsys.com
CUISINE: Italian / Neapolitan
DRINKS: Full Bar
SERVING: Lunch & Dinner
PRICE RANGE: $$$
NEIGHBORHOOD: Midtown West; Theatre District
Family-owned eatery serving Southern Italian
favorites since 1944. If you only have time for a

single meal in an Italian restaurant, you could do worse than coming here, where Frank Sinatra used to hang out quite frequently. (He had his own table as well as a private entrance.) Ask the waiter about the dishes *they don't have on the menu.* There are several. My Favorites: Fennel sausages in a marinara sauce with sweet peppers; I think the Veal Chop parmigiana is spectacular. This is food made the old fashioned way—their care and attention to consistent quality shows up on every plate of food that comes out of the kitchen. Celebrity hangout.

PIETRO'S
232 E 43rd St (Second Ave), 212-682-9760
pietros.com
CUISINE: Italian/Steakhouse
DRINKS: Full Bar
SERVING: Dinner; Closed Sun
PRICE RANGE: $$$
NEIGHBORHOOD: Midtown East; near U.N.
Old-School Italian Steakhouse serving American favorites as well. This place has been an institution since it opened in this neighborhood in 1932. (They've been in the current location since 1984.) The décor looks like they haven't changed anything in 20 years, but there's something about the blah-blah shabby look that suits the place perfectly. Menu picks: Homemade Cannelloni and Lamb Chops. Large menu and impressive wine list. If you want to try something you can't get anywhere else, get the "Shells a la Nat," a shell pasta dish served in a sublime bone marrow sauce. It's rich and deeply satisfying. (Nat was owner Pietro's brother.) While

the steaks here are wonderful, I'd opt for one of their excellent pastas.

PER SE
Time Warner Center
10 Columbus Circle, 212-823-9335
www.perseny.com
CUISINE: French
DRINKS: Full bar
SERVING: Dinner nightly, Lunch (Fri – Sun)
NEIGHBORHOOD: Midtown West
PRICE RANGE: $$$$+
Famed Chef **Thomas Keller** is behind this place, considered to be one of the best restaurants in the world. The menu is fixed, so you can expect a dizzying array of delectable masterpieces. (When you finish, the waiter will bring by a box containing handmade chocolates—they'll explain to you what the filling is in each one—a nice touch to wrap up a memorable evening.)

POLO BAR
1 E 55th St (Fifth Ave), 212-207-8562
www.ralphlauren.com
CUISINE: American (Traditional)
DRINKS: Full Bar
SERVING: Dinner, Lunch
PRICE RANGE: $$$
NEIGHBORHOOD: Midtown East
One of the posh gathering places for New York's elite is designer Ralph Lauren's lavishly decorated eatery offering a menu of classic American fare. Bar is upstairs, dining room is downstairs in the basement—

no windows, but brilliantly conceived. If you can snag a table, don't be surprised when you see celebrities. The same kind of people go here that go to the Modern, the Monkey Bar and Michael's. Chef Eric Ripert said the downstairs dining room was "the best-lighted restaurant" in New York. Menu picks: Ralph's corned beef sandwich (as famous here as the chicken hash is at the **21 Club**) and Pigs in a blanket. Nice selection of wines. Reservations required, unless you get *really* lucky and walk in to find an open table.

SARDI'S
234 W 44th St (near Broadway), 212-221-8440
www.sardis.com
CUISINE: American
DRINKS: Full Bar
SERVING: Lunch, Dinner
PRICE RANGE: $$$
NEIGHBORHOOD: Midtown West / Theatre District
This iconic restaurant, located in the heart of New York's Theater District, serves lunch and dinner every

day except Sunday and Monday. Great dining before and after the theatre and you might even see a Broadway star. It's a tradition for the cast to drop into Sardi's after their opening night performance to celebrate. Check out the famous cartoon celebrity sketches on the walls. (The upstairs bar on second floor is where I go for a drink because that's where people in the theatre go. I do all my meetings up here if I'm in the Theatre District.)

SEN SAKANA
28 W 44th St (bet. Avenue of the Americas & 5th Ave), 212-221-9560
www.sensakana.com
CUISINE: Sushi/Japanese/ Peruvian
DRINKS: Full Bar
SERVING: Lunch & Dinner; Dinner only on Sat & Sun
PRICE RANGE: $$$
NEIGHBORHOOD: Midtown West
Upscale eatery offering a large menu of Japanese-Peruvian fare including Nikkei cuisine. Picks: Acevichado Makis and Tiradito Madai. Also ceviche & sushi. Impressive bar menu.

SERRA ALPINA BY LA BIRRERIA
Eataly
200 Fifth Ave (near 24th St), 212-937-8910
Across from Madison Square Park
www.eataly.com/nyc-birreria
CUISINE: Italian
DRINKS: Beer & Wine
SERVING: Lunch, Dinner

PRICE RANGE: $
NEIGHBORHOOD: Flatiron District
This is Mario Batali's Eataly's rooftop beer bar that has a great selection of beer and wines. Food choices are fresh and tasty. Menu favorites include: Piato Misto and Roasted maitake, oyster, and white beech mushrooms, encircled by young pea shoots and topped by fresh burrata. I love their excellent sausages. Casual dining at its best with great views. Though everything else in Eataly is pretty costly, you can get away cheaper up here if you're careful. The ingredients may come from America, but the recipes are Italian. Note that there are 9 restaurants in Eataly alone, each with a distinct personality and menu of its own. You could wander in here and spend a week, never seeing anything that New York has to offer, and I'm sure that's what Mario and his backers had in mind when they opened this splendidly gargantuan place.

SPARKS STEAK HOUSE
210 E 46th St (Third Ave), 212-687-4855
sparkssteakhouse.com
CUISINE: Steakhouse
SERVING: Lunch & Dinner, Dinner only on Sat; Closed Sun
PRICE RANGE: $$$$
NEIGHBORHOOD: Midtown East
Since 1966, this family-owned steakhouse has been packing them in. It's justifiably famous as one of the great steakhouses in Manhattan. It's also quite famous among regulars for the night in December, 1985, when Gambino mob boss Big Paul Castellano was the

victim of a Mafia hit as he was getting out of his limo to go into the steakhouse. Another Gambino thug, John Gotti, ordered the hit, and watched from a nearby car as 3 men gunned down Big Paul and his driver. Big Paul loved meat and knew a lot about it (his father had been a butcher) and his favorite cut was the Porterhouse cooked medium rare with horseradish on the side. I can agree that it's my favorite cut as well, LOL. Other Favorites: Steak Fromage and Fresh Chilean Sea Bass. Extensive wine list. (When I was younger, I spent more on their full-bodied reds than I ever did on the steaks—I don't make that mistake these days.) Vegetarian options. Private party rooms.

SUSHI GINZA ONODERA
461 Fifth Ave (bet. 41st & 40th Sts), 212-390-0925
www.sushiginzaonoderanewyork.com
CUISINE: Japanese/Sushi
DRINKS: Full Bar
SERVING: Lunch & Dinner, Dinner only on Sat; closed Sunday
PRICE RANGE: $$$$
NEIGHBORHOOD: Midtown East
Upscale eatery offering omakase-only sushi. Everything is flown in from Tokyo fish market several times a week so you know it's fresh. Menu picks: Yellow jack with lemon juice and Japanese barracuda. Tasty miso soup. Tip included in price of meal.

SUSHI SEKI
365 W 46th St (bet. 9th Ave & 8th Ave), 212-262-8880
www.sushiseki.com
CUISINE: Sushi/Japanese
DRINKS: Full Bar

SERVING: Dinner; closed Sunday
PRICE RANGE: $$$
NEIGHBORHOOD: Midtown West, Hell's Kitchen, Theater District
Beautiful upscale eatery that offers a varied menu of Japanese cuisine and sushi. Downstairs has a long marble bar for drinks and lighter fare and a communal table and tasting menus. Upstairs is for sushi, private tatami rooms, a sushi bar and tables for omakase. Favorites: Uni sushi and Ootoro sashimi. Great desserts. Reservations recommended.

TEMERARIO
198 8th Ave (bet. 21st St & 20th St), 212-645-2100
www.temerarionyc.com
CUISINE: Mexican
DRINKS: Full Bar
SERVING: Lunch & Dinner; Weekend Brunch
PRICE RANGE: $$
NEIGHBORHOOD: Chelsea
Popular eatery offering a creative menu of typical Mexican street food interpreted broadly. Menu picks: Mahi Mahi fish tacos and Chorizo queso fundido topped with avocado. Happy hour specials. Tasty margaritas.

UPLAND
345 Park Ave S (bet. 26th St & 25th St), 212-686-1006
www.uplandnyc.com
CUISINE: American (New)
DRINKS: Full Bar
SERVING: Lunch & Dinner
PRICE RANGE: $$$
NEIGHBORHOOD: Flatiron
Spacious, trendy brasserie featuring a menu of American cuisine with California and Italian influences. Nice selection of pizzas, steaks, and fish dishes. The Duck special stole the show. Great cocktails and tasty desserts. (Upland is the California town where the chef is from.)

VIA BRASIL
34 W 46 St (bet. Fifth & Sixth Aves), 212-997-1158
www.viabrasilrestaurant.com
CUISINE: Brazilian

DRINKS: Full Bar
SERVING: Lunch, Dinner
PRICE RANGE: $$
NEIGHBORHOOD: Midtown
You've heard of New York's Little Italy (Nolita), Chinatown and Koreatown, right? Well, there's a Little Brazil as well. When I say little, I mean it: it's scarcely a block long and it's here in Midtown. It makes for a nice (if offbeat) place for a celebration or a business meal. Menu favorites include: Shredded baked codfish and Grilled Salmon and pineapple sauce. Brazilian specialties are tasty too, like the "feijoada completa," which is a hefty stew made of black beans and chunks of pork that's become the national dish of the country.

WOLLENSKY GRILL
210 E 49th St (bet. 2nd & 3rd Aves), 212-753-0444
https://www.smithandwollenskynyc.com/wollenskys-grill/
CUISINE: Steakhouse
DRINKS: Full bar
SERVING: Lunch & Dinner
PRICE RANGE: $$$$
NEIGHBORHOOD: Midtown East
The "regular" Smith & Wollensky is right next door, but skip it and slip into the Grill instead. Much more interesting ambience. You get all the great food you'd get at the steakhouse in a much more welcoming atmosphere. Start with a chilled whole lobster and then choose your favorite cut of steak. You can't do better than this. If you're here for lunch, try the Prime Roast Beef Hash.

Midtown
Budget Spots

2ND AVE DELI

162 E 33rd St (bet. Lexington Ave & 3rd Ave), 212-689-9000

www.2ndavedeli.com

CUISINE: Deli/Kosher

DRINKS: Beer & Wine

SERVING: Breakfast, Lunch, Dinner

PRICE RANGE: $$

NEIGHBORHOOD: Murray Hill, Kips Bay, Midtown East

Popular deli for decades known for their great overstuffed sandwiches. Yiddish theatre posters adorn the walls. Tiled floor, T-shirts, cookbooks. This is the place to get tongue and chopped liver. Of course they serve Matzoh Ball soup. Jellied calves feet.

ACUARIO CAFÉ

306 W 37th St (bet. 9th Ave & 8th Ave), 212-564-9040

www.acuariocafe.wordpress.com

CUISINE: Latin American

DRINKS: No Booze

SERVING: Breakfast & Lunch; closed Sun

PRICE RANGE: $
NEIGHBORHOOD: Midtown West, Hell's Kitchen
Located inside of a loading dock, this hole-in-the-wall café offers a menu of Latin American cuisine and attracts quite a diverse crowd (mostly blue collar working class). Favorites: Central American chicken; fried fish; beef stew; and fresh fish with rice and beans. Eat in or take-away. Cash only. Cheap & good.

BLUE BOTTLE COFFEE
1 Rockefeller Plaza, Concourse Level, 510-653-3394
www.bluebottlecoffee.com
CUISINE: Coffee & Tea
DRINKS: No Booze
SERVING: Lunch & Dinner
PRICE RANGE: $$
NEIGHBORHOOD: Rockefeller Center
Great coffeeshop with several New York locations. This one is tucked away underground on the Concourse Level located just around the corner from the ice skating rink. Serves up a variety of coffees and treats like granola, yogurt parfaits, and pastries. You can walk east underground and when you come out, you'll be in front of Saks Fifth Avenue.

CASA MONO
52 Irving Pl (bet. 18th St & 17th St), 212-253-2773
www.casamononyc.com
CUISINE: Spanish
DRINKS: Beer & Wine
SERVING: Lunch & Dinner
PRICE RANGE: $

NEIGHBORHOOD: Gramercy, Union Square, Flatiron

Intimate upscale eatery offering Spanish small-plate fare. The dining room has glass doors that push open in the summer months to give that al fresco feeling. Mosaic tile floors. Favorites: Soft shell crab; Hudson Valley duck; octopus with fennel & grapefruit; skirt steak with romesco; rabbit with habanero cuajada. Nice wine list, perhaps the best list of Spanish wines in the whole city. If you like sherry, this is definitely a place you'll want to visit. The sommeliers are very knowledgeable, and they've got lots of wines with excellent prices. Reservations recommended, though the best time to come is between lunch and dinner, when it's more intimate and not as crazy-hectic.

CHEF YU

520 8th Ave (W 37th St), 212-736-6150

www.chefyu-nyc.com/

CUISINE: Chinese

DRINKS: Full bar

SERVING: Lunch, Dinner

NEIGHBORHOOD: Midtown West / Garment District

PRICE RANGE: $$

They have 15 lunch options for less than $6. And it's all tasty. Dinner is almost as cheap: pan-fried vegetable dumplings, shrimp dumplings, minced chicken and pine nuts, 5-spice roast beef, tangerine chicken, a dozen steak plates, pork, wide variety of fish and shellfish dishes, all in the $11 to $13 range. Can't go wrong here.

HAANDI
113 Lexington Ave (bet. 27th St & 28th St), 212-685-5200
http://haandiny.com/
CUISINE: Indian/Pakistani
DRINKS: No Booze
SERVING: 10 a.m. – 4 a.m.
PRICE RANGE: $
NEIGHBORHOOD: Kips Bay
Popular cheap spot serving ready-made dishes from Southeast Asia. Favorites: Chicken kabab and Dal Gosht (mutton with lentils). No frills eatery.

HAN BAT
53 W 35th St (near Sixth Ave), 212-629-5588
www.nychanbat.com

CUISINE: Korean
DRINKS: Beer & Wine
SERVING: Lunch, Dinner
PRICE RANGE: $$
NEIGHBORHOOD: Koreatown
Very popular Korean eatery. Intimate and often crowded. This 24-hour eatery serves typical Korean fare like crispy pancakes with squid and mandoo, crispy half-moon-shaped dumplings.

HIDE-CHAN RAMEN
248 E 52nd St (Second Ave), second floor, 212-813-1800
http://www.hidechanramen.nyc/
314 W 53rd St (bet. 8th & 9th Aves), 212-969-0066
www.hidechanusa.com
CUISINE: Ramen
DRINKS: Beer & Wine
SERVING: Breakfast & Lunch; closed Sat & Sun

PRICE RANGE: $$
NEIGHBORHOOD: Theater District, Midtown West, Hell's Kitchen; also Midtown East
Small ramen shop, one on the East Side and one on the West Side, serving up favorites like black garlic noodles, pork buns & pork bone broth. Favorites: Chicken teriyaki avocado bowl and Bonito Dashi Ramen. Lunch specials. Sake cocktails and variety of beers. If you've never experienced a *real* Ramen eatery, do yourself a favor and try this one.

HILL COUNTRY CHICKEN
1123 Broadway (W 25th St), 212-257-6446
www.hillcountrychicken.com/
CUISINE: Southern
DRINKS: Beer & Wine
SERVING: Breakfast, Lunch, Dinner
NEIGHBORHOOD: Midtown South
PRICE RANGE: $$
You're coming here for fried chicken, period. Helpful staff, busy and exciting atmosphere in a fun-filled place. Bright and cheerful, with yellow being a prominent color. Cheesy mashed potatoes and don't overlook the pies.

KATSU-HAMA
11 E 47th St (Fifth Ave), 212-758-5909
katsuhama47.com
CUISINE: Tonkatsu/Japanese
DRINKS: Beer & Wine
SERVING: Lunch & Dinner
PRICE RANGE: $$
NEIGHBORHOOD: Midtown East

No-frills Japanese comfort food eatery with counter service specializing in grilled pork. Favorites: Berkshire Pork Katsu and Pork Loin Cutlet. I love the way the pork cutlet comes out resting on a little wire cage that helps stop the steam from ruining the wonderful texture of the crusty shell. And it's cheap. No Reservations.

LA BONNE SOUPE
48 W 55th St (Ave of the Americas), 212-586-7650
labonnenyc.com
CUISINE: French
DRINKS: Full Bar
SERVING: Lunch & Dinner
PRICE RANGE: $$
NEIGHBORHOOD: Midtown West
French bistro offering a simple (and highly satisfying) menu of quiche, crepes, and other classics that has been pleasing (those who know about it, at least)

since it opened in 1973. Favorites: Duck and
Escargot; I'm particularly fond of the Chicken Confit
(they slow cook the thigh); Vegan options.
Reservations recommended – quite busy.

LOS TACOS NO. 1
75 Ninth Avenue, 212-256-0343
www.lostacos1.com
CUISINE: Mexican
DRINKS: No Booze
SERVING: Lunch, Dinner
NEIGHBORGHOOD: Chelsea, Meatpacking District
PRICE RANGE: $
Located in the Chelsea Market, here you'll find
authentic tacos, Adobaba tacos, deep-fried quesadillas
and horchata. All made with hand-pressed tortillas.
Mexican beverages.

MARGON
136 W 46th St (Seventh Ave), 212-354-5013
ordermargon.com

CUISINE: Cuban
DRINKS: Beer & Wine
SERVING: Breakfast and Late Lunch
PRICE RANGE: $
NEIGHBORHOOD: Midtown West
Small Latin counter-service eatery serving authentic Cuban cuisine. Favorites: Cuban sandwich and Beef Stew. American breakfasts & salads.

MOMOSAN RAMEN & SAKE
342 Lexington Ave (39th St), 646-201-5529
www.momosanramen.com
CUISINE: Ramen
DRINKS: Full Bar
SERVING: Lunch & Dinner; Dinner only on Sunday
PRICE RANGE: $$
NEIGHBORHOOD: Murray Hill, Midtown East
Popular Ramen eatery with communal tables and an impressive selection of sakes. Favorites: Tontoksu ramen and Toppogi-rice cakes.

TAAM-TOV
41 W 47th St (Ave of the Americas), third floor, 212-768-8001
taamtovnyc.com
CUISINE: Uzbek / Middle Eastern / kosher Bukharian
DRINKS: Beer & Wine
SERVING: Lunch & Dinner; Closed Sat & Sun
PRICE RANGE: $$
NEIGHBORHOOD: Midtown West
Located in the Diamond District, you'll have to walk up a couple of floors to get to this little gem that

features a menu of Middle Easter specialties with an emphasis on Uzbek cuisine. Menu picks: Lamb Kebabs (they have about 10 Kebab selections on a very big menu) with the Uzbek rice pilaf. I get the Manty as a starter (big plumb beef dumplings). Kosher eatery so no dairy is served. Turkish coffees. Vegetarian Options.

TACUBA
802 9th Ave (55th St), 212-245-4500
www.tacubanyc.com
CUISINE: Mexican/Latin American
DRINKS: Full Bar
SERVING: Lunch & Dinner
PRICE RANGE: $$
NEIGHBORHOOD: Theater District, Hell's Kitchen, Midtown West
Popular cantina offering a great assortment of classic Mexican fare. Menu picks: Quesadilla de flor (burrata, zucchini flower, and a kale pesto) and Fried Brussels sprouts and short rib quesadilla. Large selection of Tequilas and Mezcal.

TIFFIN WALLAH
127 E 28th St, 212-685-7301
www.tiffindelivery.us
CUISINE: South Indian, Vegetarian
DRINKS: Beer & Wine
SERVING: Lunch, Dinner
NEIGHBORHOOD: Midtown East – Kips Bay
PRICE RANGE: $$
Spicy tomato lentil soup; Punjab curries; Gujarati curries; Undhiyu; Sukhi Bhaji; Dosa (large crispy crepes served with coconut chutney and sambar); Uttapam, and lots more.

Chapter 3
UPPER EAST SIDE

THE BAR ROOM
117 E 60th St (bet. Park Ave & Lexington Ave), 212-561-5523
www.thebarroomnyc.com
CUISINE: American (New)
DRINKS: Full bar
SERVING: Lunch & Dinner
PRICE RANGE: $$
NEIGHBORHOOD: Upper East Side
Stylish bistro offering a creative men of New American fare. Black-and-white checked tiles on the floor, a long highly polished wooden bar, red banquettes and café chairs all project a perfect bistro atmosphere. Picks: Lobster rolls and Salmon. Craft beer & classic cocktails. Can be busy but only takes reservations for large groups.

BOHEMIAN SPIRIT
321 East 73rd St (bet. 1st Ave & 2nd Ave), 212-861-1038
www.bohemianspiritrestaurant.com
CUISINE: Czech
DRINKS: Full Bar
SERVING: Dinner
PRICE RANGE: $$
NEIGHBORHOOD: Upper East Side, Yorkville

Popular Central European eatery with images of Czech celebrities adorning the walls. Serves a menu of Czech favorites like Schnitzel and Beef Goulash; beer roasted sausages; svickova (roasted beef in a cream sauce) with dumplings and cranberry; duck leg with red cabbage. Nice selection of Pilsner beer.

CAFÉ SABARSKY
Neue Galerie
1048 Fifth Ave (near 86th St), 212-288-0665
www.neuegalerie.org/cafesabarsky
CUISINE: German-Austrian
DRINKS: Beer & Wine Only
SERVING: Lunch & Dinner
PRICE RANGE: $$
NEIGHBORHOOD: Upper East Side
This Viennese-style café serves delicious German cuisine when usually what you get is very indifferent. I get through this hearty and heavy food by skipping the potatoes that seem to come with everything. Menu favorites include: Bavarian Sausage and Apple Strudel. Coffee drinks and desserts are out of this world (like the dark chocolate cake). Note that this place is inside the Neue Galerie, a wonderful showcase for German and Austrian art from the 20th Century, worth a special trip even if you don't eat here.

THE DAISY
1641 Second Ave (at E 85th St), 646-964-5756
www.thedaisynyc.com
CUISINE: American (New) / Gastropub / Mexican
DRINKS: Full Bar

SERVING: Dinner, Lunch on Sat & Sun
PRICE RANGE: $$
NEIGHBORHOOD: Yorkville, Upper East Side
Hip eatery offering a varied menu of American and
Mexican fare. Favorites: Salmon & Mushrooms and
Bolognese. Craft cocktails and an impressive Agave
Spirits collection. Live music. Friday night live DJ.

DANIEL
60 E 65th St, 212-288-0033
www.danielnyc.com
CUISINE: French/American
DRINKS: Full Bar
SERVING: Dinner only; Closed on Sun
PRICE RANGE: $$$$
NEIGHBORHOOD: Upper East Side
Upscale Chef Boulud eatery with an impressive menu
of French and American cuisine. Boulud came from
the Lyon region of France, and it's hard to find
anyone who serves up French cuisine better than his.
His kitchen staff is rigorously trained, as are the
servers in the front of the house. Only the best here.
(Of course, you'll pay handsomely for it.) Go with
one of the tasting menus and you can't go wrong.
Boulud started out at Le Cirque in 1986, and
gradually added American ideas to his menus before
moving on to open his own place in the 1990s. Nice
bar and lounge area. Quite formal, but not stuffy.
Note: main room requires men to wear suit jackets.
Reservations begin 2 months in advance. Presentation
and food live up to the two-star Michelin rating.

THE EAST POLE
133 E 65th St (nr. Lexington Ave), 212-249-2222
www.theeastpolenyc.com
CUISINE: American
DRINKS: Full Bar
SERVING: Dinner only, but lunch coming soon
PRICE RANGE: $$$$
NEIGHBORHOOD: Upper East Side
A lovely new place from the people at Fat Radish
down in Chinatown. Here, however, they are
ensconced in 2 brownstones and offer seating out in a
garden under a leafy canopy. The décor is mostly
black and white, very chic but no white tablecloths.
Oysters make a good starter, but try some of their
house-made pickles, or the Scotch egg and mustard or
the roasted cauliflower with curried lentils. Grilled
striped bass or chicken Kiev make good main

courses, or try my favorite, the Fennel & Fish Pie, with lobster and tarragon.

ELI'S TABLE
1413 3rd Ave (bet. 80th St & 81st St), 212-717-9798
https://www.elizabar.com/Elis-Table.aspx
CUISINE: American (New)
DRINKS: Full Bar
SERVING: Breakfast, Lunch, & Dinner
PRICE RANGE: $$
NEIGHBORHOOD: Upper East Side/Yorkville
Upscale eatery offers a menu of New American cuisine and the best thing about this place is the endless variety and the daily changes not only in the farm-to-table menu, but in the 20 or so wines by the glass they serve. They are really on top of their wine game here. Wine pours are 2.5 or 5 ounces, or buy a whole bottle. If you live in th4 city, check out their wine courses every 2 weeks. A lot of people in the wine business frequent this place. Favorites: Tuna tartare, crispy Octopus, English pea crostini, celery & parsley salad, soft shell crabs. But, as I say, everything changes daily. Creative desserts. Weekend brunch. **Eli's Market** is next door.

FELICE
1593 First Av. (at 83rd St.), 212-249-4080
1166 First Ave (at 64th St), 212-593-2223
www.felice64.com
www.felice83.com
CUISINE: Wine bar, Italian
DRINKS: Full bar
SERVING: Lunch, Dinner, Brunch
NEIGHBORHOOD: Upper East Side
PRINCE RANGE: $$$
If you can't get to Tuscany, close your eyes and inhale. This place will make you think you're over there. Fish beautifully prepared, organic chicken with bursting flavor and sliced steak. Pasta dishes are uniformly good, as is the butternut squash risotto. Every night the chef makes up a l'aperitivo which includes 3 tastings to launch your experience here. If you don't want the l'aperitivo, by all means opt for one of the crostini.

FLORA BAR
945 Madison Ave (E 75th St), 646-558-5383
www.florabarnyc.com
CUISINE: Seafood
DRINKS: Beer & Wine
SERVING: Breakfast, Lunch, Dinner
PRICE RANGE: $$
NEIGHBORHOOD: Upper East Side
Located in the **Met Breuer** in the sunken space under
the lobby, this eclectic modern eatery offers a creative
menu focusing on seafood. Favorites: Blue shrimp
with cocktail sauce; Rutabaga & raclette tart; Steak
with beets & béarnaise; Lobster crudo and Snow crab.
Nice wine selection.

FRED'S AT BARNEY'S NEW YORK
660 Madison Ave (bet. 60th and 61st Sts), 212-833-
2200
www.barneys.com
CUISINE: American/Italian
DRINKS: Full Bar
SERVING: Lunch & Dinner

PRICE RANGE: $$$
NEIGHBORHOOD: Upper East Side
Located on the ninth floor of Barney's, this is a popular place for the "ladies who lunch" crowd. Especially the younger ladies. It also attracts a big following in the fashion and media worlds. Menu favorites include: Chicken livers and Pot roast. The Lobster Club is the best, but the chopped salad is de rigueur. It's a little loud (that's why it's so fun) and reservations are recommended.

J. G. MELON

1291 Third Ave (bet. 75th St & 74th St), 212-744-0585
https://jgmelon-nyc.com
CUISINE: American (Traditional)
DRINKS: Full Bar
SERVING: Lunch & Dinner
PRICE RANGE: $$
NEIGHBORHOOD: Upper East Side, Yorkville
Comfortable neighborhood eatery known for their succulent burgers cooked on the griddle. Been here for decades. Cash only. Bobby Flay says, "I just walk in here and a burger magically appears." Good example to follow.

JEAN-GEORGES
Trump Hotel
1 Central Park West, 212-299-3900
www.jean-georges.com
CUISINE: French / American / Asian
DRINKS: Full bar
SERVING: Lunch, Dinner
NEIGHBORHOOD: Upper West Side
PRICE RANGE: $$$$; jackets required at dinner.
Flagship of **Jean-Georges Vongerichten**. I'd go with
the tasting menu either for lunch or dinner. They are
good values. (They have a 3-course tasting menu or
two 6-course menus.)

LA GOULUE
29 E 61st St, 212-988-8169
www.lagouluerestaurant.com
CUISINE: French
DRINKS: Full Bar
SERVING: Lunch & Dinner
PRICE RANGE: $$$
NEIGHBORHOOD: Upper East Side

Upscale French bistro is a treasured New York institution, in New York since the 1970s. This place even has the dark wood paneling from the original location, which was 4 blocks from here. They kept it in storage and installed it here when they had to move because the landlord forced them out. Most of the servers are French, which helps to throw off the ambiance of a "real" French bistro, though most French bistros don't have the snob factor as much as you get here. If they seat you in the rear, don't let it worry you. It just means you're a Nobody. But even so, it's quite an experience watching all the other 1-percenters show off, ruffle their feathers and preen. Favorites: I love the marinated herring here, as well as the haricots verts and the onion soup to start; Sole meunière is always a good choice; Steak tartare is always really good here, and the whole grilled Dorade. Impressive wine list. Make reservations. Much prefer this over **Le Bibloquet**, which is nearby, because there are fewer loud people making a fuss over themselves.

LE BILBOQUET
20 E 60th St (bet. Madison & Park), 212-751-3036
http://www.lebilboquetny.com/
CUISINE: French/Cajun/Creole
DRINKS: Full Bar
SERVING: Lunch & Dinner
PRICE RANGE: $$$
NEIGHBORHOOD: Upper East Side
Busy, bustling, cramped & trendy upscale eatery favored by the very wealthy, bold-faced names one sees in swanky Upper East Side bastians. Movie stars,

bigwigs in finance and media, you name it, they come here or **La Goulue** a hop and a skip away. Favorites: Cajun chicken is a must-have here; Filet, Fries and Creamed Spinach comes as one dish. The desserts are spectacular. It's hard to limit yourself to just one. Impressive wine list, but not for the faint of heart. Prices are ridiculous. Reservations recommended (not that they always honor them if it doesn't suit them). Snob factor is high.

PASTRAMI QUEEN
1125 Lexington Ave (bet. E 78th & 79th St), 212-734-1500
www.pastramiqueen.com
CUISINE: Deli/Kosher
DRINKS: No Booze
SERVING: Lunch & Dinner
PRICE RANGE: $$
NEIGHBORHOOD: Upper East Side
Kosher deli known for their overstuffed sandwiches. Pastrami (made on site), smoked turkey, corned beef – all worth tasting. Also deli classics like matzo balls and knishes. Limited seating.

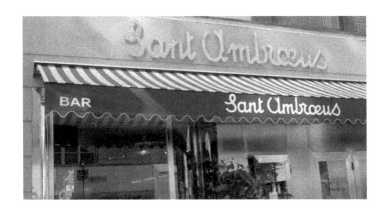

SANT AMBROEUS

1000 Madison Ave (bet. 77th & 78th Sts), 212-570-2211

www.santambroeus.com

CUISINE: Italian

DRINKS: Full Bar

SERVING: Brunch, Lunch, Dinner

PRICE RANGE: $$$

NEIGHBORHOOD: Upper East Side

A great little Italian eatery that is popular for breakfast and brunch with people in the Manhattan fashion industry. If you know who they are, you'll see a lot of famous names stroll in here for lunch. Menu favorites include: Tagliatelle in a light veal ragu and Agliatelle alla Bolognese. Great place for afternoon coffee / cappuccino and dessert. Family friendly.

SERENDIPITY 3
225 E 60th St (bet. Second & Third Aves), 212-838-3531
www.serendipity3.com
CUISINE: American, Desserts
DRINKS: No Booze
SERVING: Lunch & Dinner
PRICE RANGE: $$
NEIGHBORHOOD: Upper East Side
This iconic Upper East Side favorite of Andy Warhol still attracts crowds and there's usually a wait for tables. A favorite of kids and those who love sweets. Menu favorites are the Frozen Hot Chocolate and the giant burgers. Beyoncé and Gwyneth stop in here.

THE SIMONE
151 E 82nd St (bet. Lexington Ave & 3rd Ave), 212-772-8861
https://thesimonenyc.com
CUISINE: French
DRINKS: Full Bar
SERVING: Dinner; closed Sunday
PRICE RANGE: $$$$
NEIGHBORHOOD: Upper East Side
Upscale eatery serving classic French fare laid out on a handwritten menu. Though the atmosphere in the townhouse and the attitude of the waiters is quite formal, there's nothing stuffy about the place, nothing at all. Favorites: Duck Breast and Wild King Salmon. Delicious dessert selection. Crafted cocktails. Impressive wine list.

SISTINA
24 E 81st St (bet. 5th Ave & Madison Ave) 212-861-7660
www.sistinany.com
CUISINE: Italian
DRINKS: Full Bar
SERVING: Lunch, & Dinner; Closed Sun
PRICE RANGE: $$$$
NEIGHBORHOOD: Upper East Side
Sophisticated bistro offering a menu of classic Italian fare. Located just a block from the Metropolitan Museum of Art, it's appropriate that the walls here display Matisse and other notable artists. Don't bother looking at the menu as they always have great specials (usually around 10), and it can take the waiter more than a few minutes just to go through

them. I always order one of the specials here, never from the menu unless there's something I particularly have a yearning for, like the langoustines you can get each spring—they're grilled and seasoned beautifully. Pappardelle Sistina with veal Bolognese and wild mushrooms; Crispy-skinned branzino; Grilled octopus. Great pastas. Massive wine list.

THE WRITING ROOM
1703 Second Ave (88th St), 212-335-0075
www.thewritingroomnyc.com
CUISINE: American
DRINKS: Full bar
SERVING: Dinner
NEIGHBORHOOD: Upper East Side; Yorkville
PRICE RANGE: $$$

This is the location of the famed restaurant Elaine's, home to hundreds of writers over the decades. It closed not too long after its eponymous owner died. Now the people from Parlor Steakhouse, Michael and Susy Glick, have reopened it. It's got the same clubby feel that Elaine's had. Smoked white fish; roasted chicken soup; veal meatloaf; fried chicken (very good); smoked prime brisket.

Upper East Side
Budget Spots

BOHEMIAN SPIRIT
321 East 73rd St (bet. 1st Ave & 2nd Ave), 212-861-1038
www.bohemianspiritrestaurant.com
CUISINE: Czech
DRINKS: Full Bar
SERVING: Dinner
PRICE RANGE: $$
NEIGHBORHOOD: Upper East Side, Yorkville
Popular Central European eatery with images of Czech celebrities adorning the walls. Serves a menu of Czech favorites like Schnitzel and Beef Goulash; beer roasted sausages; svickova (roasted beef in a cream sauce) with dumplings and cranberry; duck leg with red cabbage. Nice selection of Pilsner beer.

PASTRAMI QUEEN
1125 Lexington Ave (bet. E 78th & 79th St), 212-734-1500
www.pastramiqueen.com
CUISINE: Deli/Kosher
DRINKS: No Booze
SERVING: Lunch & Dinner
PRICE RANGE: $$
NEIGHBORHOOD: Upper East Side
Kosher deli known for their overstuffed sandwiches. Pastrami (made on site), smoked turkey, corned beef – all worth tasting. Also deli classics like matzo balls and knishes. Limited seating.

PENELOPE
159 Lexington Ave (E 30th St), 212-481-3800
www.penelopenyc.com/
CUISINE: American
DRINKS: Beer & Wine
SERVING: Breakfast, Lunch, Dinner

NEIGHBORHOOD: Midtown South; Kips Bay
PRICE RANGE: $$
Charming unpretentious place in Murray Hill where I used to live. A real family atmosphere. (Penelope is their turtle.) Chicken meatballs with pesto; curried chicken salad; Ellie's spinach pie; chicken pot pie; variety of excellent sandwiches, including my favorite the BBLT (extra bacon).

SCHALLER & WEBER
1654 2nd Ave (bet. 85th St & 86th St), 212-879-3047
www.schallerweber.com
CUISINE: Meat shop
DRINKS: No Booze
SERVING: 10 a.m. – 7 p.m.; closed Sunday
PRICE RANGE: $$
NEIGHBORHOOD: Yorkville, Upper East Side
Old-school German market & butcher shop. Here you'll find a wide variety of wieners, fresh meat, cold

cuts, cheeses, jams, bread, candy, coffee and other
sundries.

TACO MIX
234 E 116th St. (bet. 2nd & 3rd Aves.), East Harlem,
212-289-2963
www.eatrealtacos.com
CUISINE: Mexican
DRINKS: No booze
SERVING: Lunch, Dinner
NEIGHBORHOOD: Upper East Side
PRICE RANGE: $
Tacos al pastor is what you want here and they're so
good they're worth a special trip.

Chapter 4
UPPER WEST SIDE

AFRICA KINE
2267 7th Ave (bet. W 133rd St & w 134th St), 212-
666-9400
www.africakinerestaurant.com/
CUISINE: Fast Food
DRINKS: No Booze
SERVING: Lunch & Dinner
PRICE RANGE: $$
NEIGHBORHOOD: Harlem
Small eatery serving a varied menu of traditional
African comfort fare. Favorites: Lamb mate; thiebou
guinaar; Dibi chicken and Lamb with plantains. There

are too many places serving this kind of food in America. Enjoy this on your visit. Women cook during lunch, while at dinner the men come in for their shift.

AMY RUTH'S
113 W 116th St (nr. Malcolm X Blvd), 212-280-8779
www.amyruths.com
CUISINE: Southern, Soul Food
DRINKS: Full Bar
SERVING: Breakfast, Lunch, Dinner daily; till 5 a.m. on weekends
PRICE RANGE: $$
Behind an unpretentious storefront you'll find this legendary Harlem eatery where they have a special called "The Rev. Al Sharpton," consisting of chicken and waffles. Braised oxtail stew; jerked chicken Jamaica style; country chicken and dumplings; smothered steak; honey-dipped friend chicken; BBQ ribs; fried or baked catfish.

BARAWINE
200 Lenox Avenue (120th Street), 646-756-4154
www.barawine.com
CUISINE: French
DRINKS: Beer & Wine Only
SERVING: Lunch, Dinner
PRICE RANGE: $$$
A beautiful French restaurant with a modern look. For starters the wine selection is great with over 200 wines and the owners are often around to offer suggestions. Menu favorites include: Tuna with seaweed salad and Duck breast. Friendly service.

BARNEY GREENGRASS
541 Amsterdam Ave (86th St), 212-724-4707
www.barneygreengrass.com
CUISINE: Deli
DRINKS: No Booze
SERVING: 8:30 a.m. – 6 p.m.
PRICE RANGE: $$
NEIGHBORHOOD: Upper West Side
In business since 1908, this iconic Jewish deli is known for their smoked fish, and a lot of other things besides. I love their scrambled eggs and omelettes. Great breakfast and sandwiches. Try the homemade Cheese Blintzes. Get the Rugelach for dessert. Cash only.

BIN 71
237 Columbus Ave. (bet. 70th & 71st St.): 212-362-5446
www.bin71.com

CUISINE: Italian/American
DRINKS: Beer & Wine Only
SERVING: Dinner
PRICE RANGE: $$
NEIGHBORHOOD: Upper West Side
This cozy wine bar and restaurant offers a comfortable atmosphere for dining or just enjoying wine or cocktails. Menu favorites include: Roasted Chicken and Meatballs. Outdoor seating available.

BOULUD SUD
20 W 64th St, 212-595-1313
www.bouludsud.com
CUISINE: Mediterranean
DRINKS: Full Bar
SERVING: Lunch & Dinner
PRICE RANGE: $$$
NEIGHBORHOOD: Upper West Side
Boulud has an inspired take on this menu of African inspired specialties. Menu favorites include: Lamb burger with Feta, Harissa, Eggplant, Tzatziki and Sweet Potato Chips. Delicious creative desserts like the Warm Lemon Custard served in a Tagine.

CALLE OCHO
2756 Broadway, 212-873-5025
www.calleochonyc.com
CUISINE: Cuban, Latin American
DRINKS: Full Bar
SERVING: Dinner & brunch on weekends
PRICE RANGE: $$
NEIGHBORHOOD: Upper West Side

Beautiful restaurant that offers a wonderful Latin experience. Here the mojitos are the best and the sangrias are amazing. The friendly servers' recommendations are usually right on. Menu favorites include: Calamari and Paella, which was abundant and fresh. For dessert try the homemade ice cream.

CHARLES' COUNTRY PAN-FRIED CHICKEN
2461 Frederick Douglass Blvd, 212-281-1800
No Website
CUISINE: Barbeque, Southern
DRINKS: No Booze
SERVING: Lunch & Dinner
PRICE RANGE: $$
NEIGHBORHOOD: Harlem
May be the best chicken north of the Mason-Dixon.

CORNER SOCIAL
321 Lenox Ave, 212-510-8552
www.cornersocialnyc.com
CUISINE: American
DRINKS: Full Bar
SERVING: Lunch & Dinner, Brunch
PRICE RANGE: $$
NEIGHBORHOOD: Harlem
Great spot for brunch with delicious offerings like Plaintain bread (a tasty take on banana bread) and Chicken and Pancakes. How about this for an artery-clogging selection: deep fried mac & cheese croquettes served with truffle mayo? Cheeseburger spring rolls? Bring 'em on. Most dishes come with free coffee. No reservations for brunch so come early.

DEAD POET
450 Amsterdam Ave. (bet. 81st & 82nd Sts.): 212-595-5670
www.thedeadpoet.com
CUISINE: Bar Snacks
DRINKS: Full Bar
SERVING: Lunch & Dinner
PRICE RANGE: $$
NEIGHBORHOOD: Upper West Side
Popular café frequented by the artsy crowd but for people watching. Good selection of beers, bottle and tap. Friendly service. Menu includes typical bar food like burgers and fries but the burgers are tasty.

EPICERIE BOULUD
1900 Broadway (bet. 63th & 64th Sts), 212-595-9606
www.epicerieboulud.com
CUISINE: Bakery, French
DRINKS: Beer & Wine Only
SERVING: Breakfast, Lunch & Dinner from 7 a.m.
PRICE RANGE: $$
NEIGHBORHOOD: Upper West Side
This modern gourmet café offers a menu that includes
everything from sandwiches and soups to cheeses and
charcuterie. Delicious desserts like pumpkin maple
pie. A great place to swing by before or after you
catch a performance at nearby Lincoln Center. A
perfect opportunity to pick up some of Daniel
Boulud's great food to-go.

GEORGE KEELEY'S
485 Amsterdam Ave. (bet. 83rd & 84th Sts.): 212-873-
0251

www.georgekeeley.com
CUISINE: American
DRINKS: Full Bar
SERVING: Late Night
PRICE RANGE: $$
NEIGHBORHOOD: Upper West Side
Popular sports bar with a friendly 30-something
crowd. Great selection of beers on tap and free
popcorn. Bar menu includes favorites like the epic
Diablo burger and garlic fries. Plenty of flat screen
TVs for watching sports. Theme nights. Friendly
service.

GIN MILL
442 Amsterdam Ave (bet. 81st & 82nd Sts): 212-
580-9080
www.nycbestbar.com
CUISINE: American
DRINKS: Full Bar
SERVING: Lunch & Dinner
PRICE RANGE: $$
NEIGHBORHOOD: Upper West Side

Popular sports bar featuring over 20 varieties of beer. Menu includes favorites like burgers, wings, and nachos. 28 large screen TVs show all the sports games. Nightly specials and ½ price happy hour.

GOOD ENOUGH TO EAT
520 Columbus Ave (at 85th St), 212-496-0163
www.goodenoughtoeat.com
CUISINE: American, Comfort food
DRINKS: Full Bar
SERVING: Open daily for Breakfast, Lunch, Dinner
PRICE RANGE: $$$$
Here in this brick-walled dining room you can find super good food. Known for executing American comfort food with exacting standards, Chef Carrie Levin offers up traditional favorites like meatloaf, grilled steaks served with mashed potatoes, a great Turkey Hash (with fresh roasted turkey, potatoes, red bell peppers, carrots, celery, 2 poached eggs and biscuits on the side). The turkey is always fresh here

because she serves a traditional Thanksgiving style turkey dinner all year-round. Her excellent breakfast selections are among the best in town (my favorite is the BLT Omelette, with double-smoked bacon, tomato and Gruyere: it's out of this world).

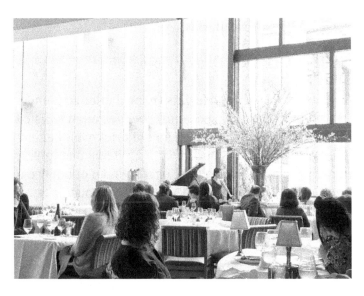

THE GRAND TIER RESTAURANT
METROPOLITAN OPERA HOUSE
30 Lincoln Center Plaza (at W 63rd St & Columbus Ave), 212-799-3400
www.patinagroup.com/restaurant.php?restaurants_id=30
CUISINE: American
DRINKS: Full Bar
SERVING: Pre-theatre and intermission dining: Mon - Sat
PRICE RANGE: $$$$

Great spot for a gourmet meal before the opera, of even if you hate opera but want to see the great lobby.

THE GRANGE BAR & EATERY

1635 Amsterdam Ave (at W 141st St), 212-491-1635
www.thegrangebarnyc.com
CUISINE: American, Bar
DRINKS: Full Bar
SERVING: Lunch, Dinner, Open daily
PRICE RANGE: $$
Located in Hamilton Heights (named after Alexander Hamilton). The 16-ounce craft beer selection is listed on a blackboard hanging on an old brick wall behind the bar. The place is decorated with items that look like they came out of a barn or attic in an old house in the Carolinas, including the weathered wood. Farm-to-table produce is a big emphasis here, with a menu featuring items like lamb sliders, fish tacos, strawberry and arugula salad; spinach ravioli, a panko-crusted Portobello mushroom burger; an organic half-roasted organic chicken with 3-herb jus, fingerling potatoes. Very cozy atmosphere.

HARLEM SHAKE

100 W. 124th St, 212-222-8300

www.harlemshakenyc.com

CUISINE: American, Burgers

DRINKS: Beer & Wine

SERVING: Lunch & Dinner

PRICE RANGE: $$

NEIGHBORHOOD: Harlem

Great burger joint that serves a classic burger and a Fatty Melt, which is two patties with cheese, pickles, special sauce and onions served on thin grilled cheese sandwiches instead of a bun. Here the food is made from fresh quality ingredients. Try the signature Harlem Shake.

JAKE'S DILEMMA

430 Amsterdam Ave. (bet. 80th & 81st Sts.): 212-580-0556

www.nycbestbar.com

CUISINE: American

DRINKS: Full Bar

SERVING: Late Night

PRICE RANGE: $$

NEIGHBORHOOD: Upper West Side

Popular neighborhood sports bar offering over 50 different US beers and 14 beers on tap.

Drink specials and half price happy hour. Foosball table and video games. Bar menu includes snacks like nachos, chicken wings, tater tots, and mozzarella sticks. Great prices and friendly crowd.

JEAN-GEORGES

Trump Hotel

1 Central Park West, New York: 212-299-3900

www.jean-georgesrestaurant.com/

CUISINE: French / American / Asian

DRINKS: Full bar

SERVING: Lunch, Dinner

NEIGHBORHOOD: Upper West Side

PRICE RANGE: $$$$; jackets required at dinner.

Flagship of **Jean-Georges Vongerichten**. I'd go with the tasting menu either for lunch or dinner. They are good values. (They have a 3-course tasting menu or two 6-course menus.

LE BOITE EN BOIS

75 W 68th St (bet. Central Park West & Columbus Ave), 212-874-2705

www.laboitenyc.com

CUISINE: French

DRINKS: Full Bar

SERVING: Lunch & Dinner

PRICE RANGE: $$$

NEIGHBORHOOD: Upper West Side

Longtime neighborhood favorite serving classic French bistro fare. Favorites: Escargot and Veal Scaloppini. Offers a pre-theater menu. 3 blocks from Lincoln Center.

LION'S HEAD TAVERN

995 Amsterdam Ave. (109th St.): 212-866-1030

www.lionsheadnyc.com

CUISINE: Bar

DRINKS: Full Bar

SERVING: Bar Snacks
PRICE RANGE: $
NEIGHBORHOOD: Manhattan Valley
Very popular dive sports bar that has great drink deals. Happy hour runs late. Eclectic mix of the under-30 crowd. Bar menu of typical snacks like wings and tater tots.

MAISON HARLEM
341 St Nicholas Ave (bet. 128th St & 127th St), 212-222-9224
www.maisonharlem.com
CUISINE: French
DRINKS: Full Bar
SERVING: Breakfast, Lunch & Dinner
PRICE RANGE: $$
NEIGHBORHOOD: Harlem
French bistro serving classics. People gather in the buzzy bar before going to the back of the room and up a couple of steps into the dining room. Though the leather booths in the back offer more privacy, I like to grab a table at the front so I can look down at the bustling bar scene. Favorites: Sea Bass and Merguez de Barbes (grilled spicy homemade lamb sausages). Great choice for breakfast.

MELBA'S
300 W 114th St (at Frederick Douglass Blvd), 212-864-7777
www.melbasrestaurant.com
CUISINE: Southern, American (Traditional), Soul Food
DRINKS: Full Bar

SERVING: Dinner nightly; brunch weekends
PRICE RANGE: $$
NEIGHBORHOOD: Harlem
Great comfort soul food restaurant with delicious dishes like BBQ turkey meatloaf served with candy yams and garlic mash potatoes. Popular spot for brunch with selections like the Eggnog Waffle. The salmon croquettes with grits is an excellent choice. Opened by Melba Wilson in 2005, she describes herself as Harlem "born, bred and buttered." (She previously worked at **Sylvia's**.

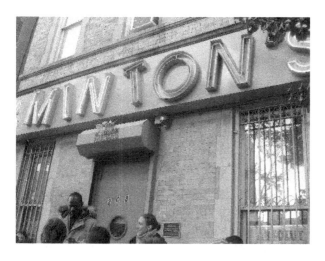

MINTON'S
206 W 118th St (near Adam Clayton Powell Blvd), 212-243-2222
www.mintonsharlem.com
CUISINE: American; Southern
DRINKS: Full Bar
SERVING: Dinner nightly from 5:30
PRICE RANGE: $$$

This jazz club offers an excellent menu to go with the live jazz performed nightly. Low Country Seafood platter gives you a tasting of blue crab fritter, crawfish hushpuppy and fried oysters. She crab soup with sherry is my absolute favorite—there's almost nowhere you can get it in Manhattan. If you're feeling particularly decadent, get the smothered lobster and crab meat casserole. You'll need a crane to lift you out of your chair. This is a great place to come if the **Cecil**, located just next door, is really busy.

MOMOFUKU MILK BAR

561 Columbus Ave (at 87th St), 212-256-0586
www.milkbarstore.com
CUISINE: Bakery, Ice Cream & Frozen Yogurt
DRINKS: No Booze
SERVING: Desserts
PRICE RANGE: $$
NEIGHBORHOOD: Upper West Side
Super cool place to stop in for a treat. Very creative things going on in here. This dessert specialty shop offers a variety of freshly baked cookies, cakes and pies. Popular items include the Confetti Cookie and Cornflake Baking Mixes. Specialty favorites include Cereal Milk (milk that tastes like it was poured from a bowl of cereal). Small lunch menu available. Novelty items for sale like T-shirts, bags, and cookbooks.

NICE MATIN

201 W 79th St (at Amsterdam Ave): 212-873 6423
www.nicematinnyc.com
CUISINE: French
DRINKS: full bar

SERVING: breakfast (from 7 a.m.), lunch, dinner
NEIGHBORHOOD: Upper West Side
PRICE RANGE: $$
This neighborhood place, good for any meal of the day, is inspired by the food from the south of France, though it's mostly American. It's reasonable, has a superior wine list with great bargains, and the food is as good as anywhere else from a great chef, **Andy D'Amico.** You'd be a regular here if you lived around the corner.

NOUGATINE AT JEAN-GEORGES
1 Central Park West (at 59th St & Columbus Circle), 212-299-3900
www.jean-georgesrestaurant.com/nougatine-and-terrace-at-jean-georges
CUISINE: French
DRINKS: Full Bar
SERVING: Breakfast, Lunch, Dinner daily
PRICE RANGE: $$$
You get a picture perfect view of Central Park at street level through the floor-to-ceiling windows at this little sleek and modern island of tranquility at Jean-Georges. The outdoor Terrace is perfect when

the weather's good. Both Nougatine and the Terrace offer less formal cuisine than the Jean-Georges, but it's just as good in a less fussy atmosphere. Foie fras brule, peekytoe crab cake; rigatoni with meatballs; roasted Dover sole.

PASHA RESTAURANT
70 W 71st St (between W Central park & Columbus Ave), 212-579-8751 www.pashanewyork.com
CUISINE: Turkish
DRINKS: Full Bar
SERVING: Lunch & Dinner
PRICE RANGE: $$
NEIGHBORHOOD: Upper West Side
A quaint restaurant with a comfortable ambiance that serves a regal menu of authentic Turkish cuisine. Menu favorites include: Octopus salad and Charcoal Grilled lamb medallions. Interesting wine list. Excellent service.

PER SE
Time Warner Center
10 Columbus Circle, New York: 212-823-9335
www.perseny.com
CUISINE: French
DRINKS: Full bar
SERVING: Dinner nightly, Lunch (Fri – Sun)
NEIGHBORHOOD: Midtown West
PRICE RANGE: $$$$+

View of Columbus Circle from Per Se

Famed Chef **Thomas Keller** is behind this place, considered to be one of the best restaurants in the world. The menu is fixed, so you can expect a dizzying array of delectable masterpieces. (When you finish, the waiter will bring by a box containing handmade chocolates—they'll explain to you what the filling is in each one—a nice touch to wrap up a memorable evening.)

PIER i CAFÉ
500 W 70th St (at Riverside Blvd), 212-362-4450
www.piericafe.com
CUISINE: American
DRINKS: Full Bar
SERVING: Lunch, Dinner, Open daily
PRICE RANGE: $$

Way up here tucked beneath the elevated West Side Highway by Riverside Park you'll find a little spot that you'd think would never make sense given where it's located. But the luscious burgers served here complement the extraordinary sunsets visible from this unique perspective.

PROHIBITION
503 Columbus Ave. (bet. 84th & 85th Sts): 212-579-3100
www.prohibition.net
CUISINE: Seafood
DRINKS: Beer & Wine Only
SERVING: Lunch & Dinner
PRICE RANGE: $$
NEIGHBORHOOD: Upper West Side
This upscale bar and lounge features live music nightly covering a variety of musical genres from groovy funk to jazz. Cool décor and funky atmosphere, this popular bar serves classic cocktails from the Prohibition era and a variety of specially drinks. Menu features New American favorites like the sombrero salad with spinach, shrimp, corn, and jalapeno cheese. No cover charge.

RED ROOSTER
310 Lenox Ave, 212-792-9001
www.redroosterharlem.com
CUISINE: Soul Food, American
DRINKS: Full Bar
SERVING: Lunch & Dinner
PRICE RANGE: $$$
NEIGHBORHOOD: Harlem

This attractive eatery serves comfort food that reflects the diverse traditions of the neighborhood. Menu

favorites include: Chicken and waffles; Catfish; fried green tomatoes served with iceberg lettuce, bacon and buttermilk dressing; dirty rice and shrimp. This place attracts a very New York mix of the trendy as well as tourists. The chef, Marcus Samuelsson, was born in Ethiopia, but he was raised in Sweden, so he's got some interesting twists on almost every dish. (He worked at the highly acclaimed Aquavit.) For dessert order the donuts or the dark chocolate cheesecake. Impressive wine list.

SARABETH'S WEST
423 Amsterdam Ave (between 80th & 81st Sts), 212-496-6280
www.sarabethsrestaurants.com/upper-west-side
CUISINE: American
DRINKS: Full Bar

SERVING: Breakfast, Lunch & Dinner
PRICE RANGE: $$
NEIGHBORHOOD: Upper West Side
A popular spot famous for its brunch, this comfortable eatery has been serving up home-style cooking for nearly 30 years. Menu favorites include: Almond crusted French toast and the Pumpkin Waffle. Expect a wait if you go on the weekend.

SHALEL LOUNGE
65 W. 70th St., downstairs (bet. Columbus Ave. & CPW): 212-873-2300
https://shalel.kitchen/
CUISINE: Moroccan
DRINKS: Full Bar
SERVING: Late Night
PRICE RANGE: $$
NEIGHBORHOOD: Upper West Side
A Moroccan-inspired lounge located downstairs giving it a cavernous feel. Romantic atmosphere is suitable for a date. Impressive wine selection. Menu favorites include: Moroccan lamb in phyllo dough. Private rooms available.

THE SMITH
1900 Broadway (at W 63rd St), 212-496-5700
www.thesmithnyc.com
CUISINE: American
DRINKS: Full Bar
SERVING: Breakfast, Lunch, Dinner, Open Daily,
PRICE RANGE: $$
While the 50-foot-long zinc-topped bar is a big
attraction, even bigger is the swell crowd that pushes
into this place after work and before the theatre.

SYLVIA'S
328 Malcolm X Blvd, 212-996-0660
www.sylviasrestaurant.com
CUISINE: Soul Food, Seafood
DRINKS: Full Bar
SERVING: Lunch & Dinner
PRICE RANGE: $$
NEIGHBORHOOD: Harlem
Named after Sylvia Woods, the "Queen of Soulfood," Sylvia's certainly lives up to the reputation. Great selection of soul food and good home cooking with delicious sides like Candied yams and Mac & Cheese. Dine at the counter or in the dining area. Very popular Sunday brunch spot but arrive early if you want a table. Though Woods died in 2012, the place is as popular as ever. The Rev. Al Sharpton said he'd dined here with everybody from President Obama to Caroline Kennedy.

TAVERN ON THE GREEN
67 Central Park W (67ᵗʰ St), 212-877-8684
www.tavernonthegreen.com
CUISINE: Steakhouse/American (New)
DRINKS: Full Bar
SERVING: Lunch & Dinner, Weekend brunch
PRICE RANGE: $$$
NEIGHBORHOOD: Central Park

Restored Central Park icon serving a menu of American fare with 700 seats sprawling out over several rooms. No one who's ever been here in the old days will ever forget it. One night I particularly remember was in the Crystal Room on a snowy night—the image of the snow gently falling outside with hundreds of white twinkling lights in the trees was spellbinding. That was then—this is now. Menu picks: Beef Carpaccio and Salmon & Scallops. Popular spot for brunch, though the food is decidedly unspectacular. The setting, however, very much is. Nice cocktails and wine selection. Reservations recommended. Great view of the park.

TESSA
349 Amsterdam Ave (W 77th St), 212-390-1974
http://tessanyc.com/
CUISINE: American, French, Italian
DRINKS: Full Bar
SERVING: Lunch, Dinner & Late Night
PRICE RANGE: $$$
The new industrial styled eatery run by Chef Cedric Tovar, formerly of Peacock Alley, serves French-Mediterranean cuisine.

VIAND
2130 Broadway (at 75th St) 212-877-2888
www.viandnyc.com/
CUISINE: Coffeeshop
DRINKS: Full Bar
SERVING: Lunch & Dinner
PRICE RANGE: $$

NEIGHBORHOOD: Upper West Side
A small diner with a counter and small two-person booths serves typical diner cuisine, but of very high quality and cheap prices. Menu favorites include the create-your-own omelette, the super deli sandwiches (the hot open-faced roast beef sandwich is great) and burgers. Crowded. No bathroom.

Upper West Side
Budget Spots

AFRICA KINE
2267 7th Ave (bet. W 133rd St & w 134th St), 212-666-9400
www.africakine.com
CUISINE: Fast Food
DRINKS: No Booze
SERVING: Lunch & Dinner
PRICE RANGE: $$
NEIGHBORHOOD: Harlem
Small eatery serving a varied menu of traditional African comfort fare. Favorites: Lamb mate; thiebou guinaar; Dibi chicken and Lamb with plantains. There are too many places serving this kind of food in America. Enjoy this on your visit. Women cook during lunch, while at dinner the men come in for their shift.

EL MALECON

764 Amsterdam Ave. (bet. 97th St. & 98th St.), 212-864-5648

www.maleconrestaurants.com

CUISINE: Latin American, Caribbean; Dominican
DRINKS: Beer & Wine
SERVING: Lunch, Dinner
NEIGHBORHOOD: Upper West Side / Manhattan Valley

PRICE RANGE: $

Good cheap Latin food. Especially good rotisserie chicken. Mofongo (smashed plantains) with shrimp is a winner.

GRAY'S PAPAYA

2090 Broadway (W 72nd St), 212-799-0243
CUISINE: Hot Dogs/Smoothies
DRINKS: No Booze
SERVING: 24 hours
PRICE RANGE: $
NEIGHBORHOOD: Upper West Side

This popular chain of all-hot dog stands has been serving NYC forever. Grab a hot dog and a papaya beverage.

THE HANDPULLED NOODLE
3600 Broadway (W 148th St), 917-262-0213
www.thehandpullednoodle.com
CUISINE: China (northwest area)
DRINKS: No Booze
SERVING: Lunch & Dinner
PRICE RANGE: $
NEIGHBORHOOD: Harlem / Hamilton Heights
Funky storefront eatery offering a variety menu of noodles and dumplings. Favorites: Dapanji (a beautifully fragrant stew anchored by chicken on the bone and lots of cardamom); Drunken noodles and Mama's Jumbo Lamb & Carrot Dumplings. Delivery available.

HILL COUNTRY CHICKEN
1123 Broadway, New York: 212-257-6446
www.hillcountrychicken.com/
CUISINE: Southern
DRINKS: Beer & Wine
SERVING: Breakfast, Lunch, Dinner
NEIGHBORHOOD: Midtown South
PRICE RANGE: $$
You're coming here for fried chicken, period. Helpful staff, busy and exciting atmosphere in a fun-filled place. Bright and cheerful, with yellow being a prominent color. Cheesy mashed potatoes and don't overlook the pies.

LA SAVANE

239 W 116th St (bet. 7th Ave & St Nicholas Ave), 646-490-4644

http://www.lasavanerestaurant.com/

CUISINE: West African / Ivorian / Pan African

DRINKS: No Booze

SERVING: Lunch & Dinner

PRICE RANGE: $

NEIGHBORHOOD: Harlem

Simple eatery serving authentic West African cuisine. There's a beautiful mural painted on the all depicting villagers near their thatched roof houses tending to a giant cauldron in the middle of the village. Nothing fancy. They don't even have knives. On a weekend night you'll see people from different countries speaking French and English. Unlike you, they won't look at the menu when they order. Favorites: Lamb shanks exceeding tasty; Guinea fowl cut into pieces and deep fried; grilled lamb with oil and sautéed onions slathered over it. Be careful when you use the hot sauce here—it's eye-watering.

LOLO'S SEAFOOD SHACK

303 W 116th St (Frederick Douglass Blvd), 646-649-3356

www.lolosseafoodshack.com

CUISINE: Seafood/Sandwiches

DRINKS: Beer & Wine

SERVING: Lunch & Dinner

PRICE RANGE: $

NEIGHBORHOOD: Harlem

Small counter-order eatery serving Caribbean-inspired fare, seafood, and sandwiches. There is a small dining room in the back of the house. (A "lolo" is an outdoor BBQ pit or roadside stand found in the West Indies.) Picks: Conch Fritters using rice flour that lightens them up a bit; Smelts deep-fried & served over plantains; Plantain Johnny Cake sandwich (perfect). Outdoor seating in the decked over yard out in the rear, weather permitting.

SAFARI

219 W 116th St, (bet. 7th Ave & St Nicholas Ave), 646-964-4252

www.safariharlem.com

CUISINE: East African / Somali

DRINKS: No Booze; good selection of juices

SERVING: Lunch & Dinner

PRICE RANGE: $$

NEIGHBORHOOD: Harlem

Laid-back café serving Somali and East African fare. This part of town houses the largest concentration of West African immigrants, so there are lots of places to eat that offer most Americans food they've never tasted before. But since Somalia is across the African continent, the food here isn't reflective of the West African cuisines you'll find in this neighborhood. Known as the first and only Somali eatery in NYC. Favorites: Beef & chicken sambusa and Chicken suqaar (spicy chicken stew with basmati rice). Chicken dishes are the best, but the goat (roasted for 6 hours) is excellent. Teas and homemade juice.

TOM'S RESTAURANT

2880 Broadway (bet. 112th St & 111th St), 212-864-6137

www.tomsrestaurant.net

CUISINE: Diner

DRINKS: No Booze

SERVING: Breakfast, Lunch & Dinner: open 24 hours Thurs-Sat

PRICE RANGE: $

NEIGHBORHOOD: Morningside Heights

Local coffee shop known for its cameo on TV show "Seinfeld." Typical diner food. Burgers, sandwiches, Chicken parm. Photos from the iconic TV show adorn the walls. Cash only.

INDEX

Lightning Source UK Ltd.
Milton Keynes UK
UKHW021530111122
411987UK00009BA/916

9 798201 046804